WHO DEFENDED THE COUNTRY?

WHO DEFENDED THE COUNTRY?

ELAINE SCARRY

EDITED BY JOSHUA COHEN AND JOEL ROGERS
A *BOSTON REVIEW* BOOK

BEACON PRESS
BOSTON

BEACON PRESS
25 Beacon Street
Boston, Massachusetts 02108-2892
www.beacon.org

Beacon Press books
are published under the auspices of
the Unitarian Universalist Association of Congregations.

07 06 05 04 03   8 7 6 5 4 3 2 1

This book is printed on acid-free paper that meets the uncoated paper
ANSI/NISO specifications for permanence as revised in 1992.

Composition by Wilsted & Taylor Publishing Services

Library of Congress Cataloging-in-Publication Data
Who defended the country? / [presented by] Elaine Scarry ;
edited by Joshua Cohen and Joel Rogers.
    p.   cm. — (New democracy forum)
Includes bibliographical references.
  ISBN 0-8070-0457-X (alk. paper)
  1. National security—United States. 2. United States—Military policy.
3. September 11 Terrorist Attacks, 2001. I. Scarry, Elaine. II. Cohen, Joshua.
III. Rogers, Joel. IV. Series.
UA23.W4553 2003
355'.033073—dc21
                                        2003001660

CONTENTS

EDITORS' PREFACE

JOSHUA COHEN AND JOEL ROGERS

The terrorism of September 11 demonstrated, most everyone agrees, that something is wrong with American security policy. But how best to understand the deficiencies and correct them? One proposed remedy is to root out the troubles by invading Iraq and adopting an aggressive policy of "preventive" war against other "threats." Another proposal (not inconsistent with the first) is to increase domestic security by putting citizens and noncitizens alike under a more watchful eye. Both strategies will lead to greater concentration of authority, more secrecy, and less democracy. And there is no guarantee that they will improve our security.

In her lead essay in this New Democracy Forum, Elaine Scarry offers a stark challenge to these conventional responses to September 11. She proposes an alternative security strategy–a more egalitarian, democratic, bottom-up approach to national defense, with greater reliance on the initiative of ordinary citizens. Scarry's proposal resonates with older ideas about the importance of an active people in ensuring national security–ideas that are commonly regarded as irrelevant in the world of modern warfare. But, focusing on the contrast between the crash of American

Flight 77 into the Pentagon and the crash of United Flight 93 in Pennsylvania, Scarry builds a forceful case for their continuing relevance. The former demonstrated the failure of conventional, top-down security arrangements, which were unable even to protect the Defense Department. The latter was a success of citizen defense. And not of citizens defending themselves: in Scarry's telling, the passengers on Flight 93 effectively mobilized through discussion and agreement to defend the country itself from attack, and their inspiring efforts produced the only successful defense on that terrible day.

Does the contrast between these two cases really suggest a more general lesson about national security strategy? And what might a more democratic approach to national security imply, outside the special case of protection against aerial attack? To feel the full force of Scarry's argument, and to join the debate on these essential questions, read on.

1

WHO DEFENDED THE COUNTRY?

ELAINE SCARRY

For the past year, we have spoken unceasingly about the events of September 11, 2001. But one aspect of that day has not yet been the topic of open discussion: the difficulty we had as a country defending ourselves; as it happened, the only successful defense was carried out not by our professional defense apparatus but by the passengers on Flight 93, which crashed in Pennsylvania. The purpose of this essay is to examine that difficulty, and the one success, and ask if they suggest that something in our defense arrangements needs to be changed. Whatever the ultimate answer to that question, we at least need to ask it since defending the country is an obligation we all share.

Speed and Security

The difficulty of defense on September 11 turned in large part on the pace of events. We need to look carefully at the timelines and timetables on that day. But as we do, it is crucial to recall that the word "speed" did not surface for the first time on September 11. It has been at the center of discussions of national defense for the last fifty years. When we look to any of our literatures on the subject, we find in the foreground statements about the speed of our weapons, of our weapons' delivery systems, and of the deliberations that will lead to their use.

Throughout this period, the heart of our defense has been a vast missile system, all parts of which are described as going into effect in "a matter of minutes": a presidential decision must be made in "a matter of minutes"; the presidential order must be transmitted in "a matter of minutes"; the speed of the missile launch must be carried out "in a matter of minutes"; and the missile must reach its target in "a matter of minutes."

The matter-of-minutes claim is sometimes formally folded into the names of our weapons (as in the Minuteman missile) and other times appears in related banner words such as "supersonic" and "hairtrigger."[1] Thousands of miles separating countries and continents can be contracted by "supersonic" missiles and planes that carry us there in "a matter of minutes"; and thousands of miles separating countries and continents can be contracted by focusing on the distance that has to be crossed not by the weapon itself but by the hand gesture that initiates the launch—the distance of a hair.

"Speed" has occupied the foreground not only of our *descriptive* statements about our national defense but also our *normative* statements. Our military arrangements for defending the country have often been criticized for moving increasingly outside the citizenry's control. The constitutional requirement for a congressional declaration of war has not been used for any war since World War II: the Korean War, the Vietnam War, and the war in former Yugoslavia were all carried out at the direction of the president and without a congressional declaration, as were the invasions of Panama, Grenada, and Haiti.[2] Speed has repeatedly been invoked to counter ethical, legal, or constitutional objections to the way our weapons policies and arrangements have slipped further and further beyond democratic structures of self-governance.

This bypassing of the Constitution in the case of conventional wars and invasions has been licensed by the existence of nuclear weapons and by the country's formal doctrine of Presidential First Use, which permits the president, acting alone, to initiate nuclear war.[3] Since the president has genocidal injuring power at his personal disposal, obtaining Congress's permission for much lesser acts of injury (as in conventional wars) has often struck presidents as a needless bother.[4] The most frequent argument used to excuse the setting aside of the Constitution is that the pace of modern life simply does not allow time for obtaining the authorization of Congress, let alone the full citizenry. Our ancestors who designed the Constitution—so the argument goes—simply had no picture of the supersonic speed at which the country's defense would need to take place. So the congressional requirement is an anachronism. With planes and weapons traveling faster than the speed of sound, what sense does it make to have a lot of sentences we have no time to hear?

Among the many revelations that occurred on September 11 was a revelation about our capacity to act quickly. Speed—the realpolitik that has excused the setting aside of the law for fifty years—turns out not to have been very *real* at all. The description that follows looks at the timetables of American Airlines Flight 77—the plane that hit the Pentagon—and United Airlines Flight 93—the plane that crashed in Pennsylvania when passengers successfully disabled the hijackers' mission. Each of the two planes was a small piece of U.S. ground. Their juxtaposition indicates that a form of defense that is external to the ground that needs to be defended does not work as well as a form of defense that is internal to the ground that needs to be protected. This outcome precisely matches the arguments that were made at the time of the writing of the Constitution about why the military had to be "held within a civil frame": about why military actions, whether offensive or defensive, must be measured against the norms of civilian life, must be brought into contact with the people with whom one farms or performs shared labor, or the people with whom one raises children, or the people with whom one goes to church or a weekly play or movie. Preserving such a civil frame was needed to prevent the infantilization of the country's population by its own leaders, and because it was judged to be the only plausible way actually to defend the home ground.

When the plane that hit the Pentagon and the plane that crashed in Pennsylvania are looked at side by side, they reveal two different conceptions of national defense: one model is authoritarian, centralized, top down; the other, operating in a civil frame, is distributed and egalitarian. Should anything be inferred from the fact that the first form of defense failed and the second succeeded? This outcome obligates us to review our military structures, and to consider the possibility that we need a democratic, not a top-down, form of defense. At the very least, the events of September 11 cast doubt on a key argument that, for the past fifty years, has been used to legitimize an increasingly centralized, authoritarian model of defense—namely the argument based on speed.

American Flight 77

American Airlines Flight 77 was originally scheduled to fly from Washington to Los Angeles. The plane approached the Pentagon at a speed of 500 miles per hour.[5] It entered the outermost of the building's five rings, ring E, then cut through ring D and continued on through ring C, and eventually stopped just short of ring B.[6] Two million square feet were damaged or destroyed.[7] Before September 11, the Pentagon was five corridors deep, five stories high, and in its overall shape, five-sided. Three of the Pentagon's five sides were affected (one had to be leveled and rebuilt; the other two were badly damaged by smoke and water).

One hundred and eighty-nine people died—64 on the plane, 125 working in the Pentagon. Many others were badly burned.[8] Thousands of people work in the Pentagon.[9] Two factors prevented many more people from being killed or badly burned. First, the building is stacked horizontally, not vertically like the World Trade Center towers—it is built like layers of sedimentary rock that have been turned on their side and lie flush with the ground. Second, one of the sections hit was being renovated and was therefore relatively empty of people when the plane entered.

While we continue to lament the deaths and injuries, and while we continue to find solace in the fact that the number of deaths and injuries was not higher, one key fact needs to be held on to and stated in a clear sentence: on September 11, the Pentagon could not defend the Pentagon, let alone the rest of the country.

The U.S. military had precious little time to respond on September 11 (and this fact has been accurately acknowledged by almost everyone, both inside and outside the country, who has spoken about the day). But by the standards of speed that have been used to justify setting aside constitutional guarantees for the last fifty years, the U.S. military on September 11 had a luxurious amount of time to protect the Pentagon. They had more than minutes. The pilots of the F-15s and F-16s that flew on September 11 made no mistakes, displayed no inadequacies, and showed no lack of courage—but what they tried to do now appears to have been a structural impossibility.

One hour and twenty-one minutes go by between the moment FAA controllers learn that multiple planes have been taken and the moment the Pentagon is struck. Controllers hear the hijackers on the first seized plane (American Flight 11) say "we have some planes" at 8:24 A.M., a sentence indicating that the plane from which the voice comes is not the sole plane presently imperiled. The information that "some planes" have been taken is available one hour and 21 minutes before the Pentagon is hit by the third seized plane at 9:45 A.M.[10]

Fifty-eight minutes go by between the attack on the first World Trade Tower (at 8:47 A.M.) and the crash into the Pentagon (9:45 A.M.). This means that for almost one hour before the Pentagon is hit, the military knows that the hijackers have multiple planes and that those hijackers have no intention to land those planes safely.

The crash of American Flight 77 into the Pentagon comes fifty-five minutes after that plane has now itself disappeared from radio contact (at 8:50 A.M.). So for *fifty-five minutes*, the military now knows three things:

1. the hijackers have multiple planes;

2. the hijackers—far from having any intention of landing the planes safely—intend to injure as many people on the ground as possible;[11] and

3. Flight 77 has *a chance* of being one of those planes since it has just disappeared from radio.

When, six minutes later, the plane loses its transponder (so that its radar image as well as its radio contact is now lost), the chance that it is one of the seized planes rises.

By the most liberal reading, then, the country had *one hour and twenty-one minutes* to begin to respond. By the most conservative reading, the country had *fifty-five minutes* to begin to respond.[12] The phrase "begin to respond" does not mean that an F-15 or F-16 could now attack the plane that would hit the Pentagon. At the one hour and twenty-one-minute clock time, the plane that will eventually hit the Pentagon is only four minutes into its flight and has not yet been hijacked. It means instead that a warning threshold has just been crossed and a level of readiness might therefore begin: at one hour and twenty-one minutes, fighter pilots could be placed on standby on the ground with engines running; at fifty-five minutes, fighter planes could be following the third plane, as well as any other planes that are wildly off course with radio contact missing.

One hour and twenty-one minutes and *fifty-five minutes* are each a short time—a short, short time. But . . . by the timetables that we have for decades accepted as descriptive of our military weapons, by the timetables we have accepted as explanations for why we must abridge our structures of self-governance—by the intoxicating timetables of "rapid response," the proud specifications of eight minutes, twelve minutes, four minutes, one minute—by these timetables, the September 11 time periods of one hour and twenty-one minutes or of fifty-five minutes are very long periods indeed.

The transition from the moment Flight 77's radio is off (at 8:50 A.M.) to the moment it disappears from secondary radar (8:56 A.M.) is crucial, for it begins to confirm the inference that this is one of the hijacked planes.[13] A sequence of confirmations now follows. While the FAA controllers have been unable to reach the plane, now the airline company also discovers its inability to reach Flight 77 on a separate radio (shortly after 9 A.M.).[14] At 9:25 a passenger, Barbara Olson, places a phone call to her husband in the U.S. Justice Department, Theodore Olson, stating that the plane is under the control of hijackers.[15] Because the passenger is well known to the Justice Department listener, no time need be lost assessing the honesty and accuracy of the report. This means that twenty minutes prior to the moment the Pentagon is hit, the Justice Department has direct, reliable voice confirmation of the plane's seizure.

So for *twenty minutes* prior to the hitting of the Pentagon, the military is in the position to know three things (the third of which differs decisively from what it knew at the fifty-five-minute marker):

1. the hijackers have multiple planes;

2. the hijackers intend to injure as many people as possible;

3. Flight 77 is *certainly* one of the hijacked planes: it has disappeared from radio, has disappeared from secondary radar, has disappeared from the company

radio, and has been described to the Justice Department as "hijacked" by a passenger whose word cannot be doubted.

The steadily mounting *layers of verification* listed in number 3 continue. At 9:33 A.M., an FAA air traffic controller sees on radar a "fast moving blip" (or "fast moving primary target") making its way toward Washington airspace: this level of verification comes *twelve minutes* prior to the plane's crash into the Pentagon. At 9:36 A.M. an airborne C-130 sees the plane itself and identifies it as a "757 moving low and fast."[16] This further confirmation comes *nine minutes* prior to the collision. No one can suppose that in nine minutes planes could be scrambled and reach the hijacked plane (even if we have, for decades, listened dutifully to descriptions of much more complicated military acts occurring in nine minutes). But certainly the layers of alert, of scrambling, of takeoff, of tracking, could have begun one hour and twenty minutes earlier, or fifty-five minutes earlier, not nine minutes earlier. Nine minutes is presumably the time frame in which only the last act of military defense need be carried out by the fighter planes—if there is any reasonable last act to be taken, a question to which I will return.

During much of its flight, American Flight 77 was over countryside (rather than over densely populated urban areas).[17] The six successive layers of verification need to be spatially displayed so that we can begin to picture where the plane was during each of them:

- loss of radio (55 minutes remain)
- loss of transponder (49 minutes remain)
- loss of contact with the airline company (approximately 36 minutes remain)
- a passenger calls the Justice Department (20 minutes remain)
- a radar image is seen moving toward Washington whose source is not using its official "secondary" radar (12 minutes remain)
- a C-130 sights a Boeing 757 flying fast and low (9 minutes remain)

Assuming an airspeed of 500 miles an hour, we can infer that at the time we learn that both the radio and the transponder are off (*the second layer of confirmation*), the plane would be 410 miles from Washington with many miles of sparsely populated land beneath it.[18] By *the fourth confirmation* (Barbara Olson's phone call), it would be 166 miles from Washington. By *the sixth confirmation,* that given by the C-130, the plane destined for the Pentagon would still be 75 miles from Washington and the possibility of minimizing injury to those on the ground would be rapidly vanishing with each passing mile.

Again, the point here is not to say, "Why couldn't these airmen shoot down the plane?" Time made that extremely difficult. But much smaller units of time have been invoked to explain our battle readiness over the last fifty years and to

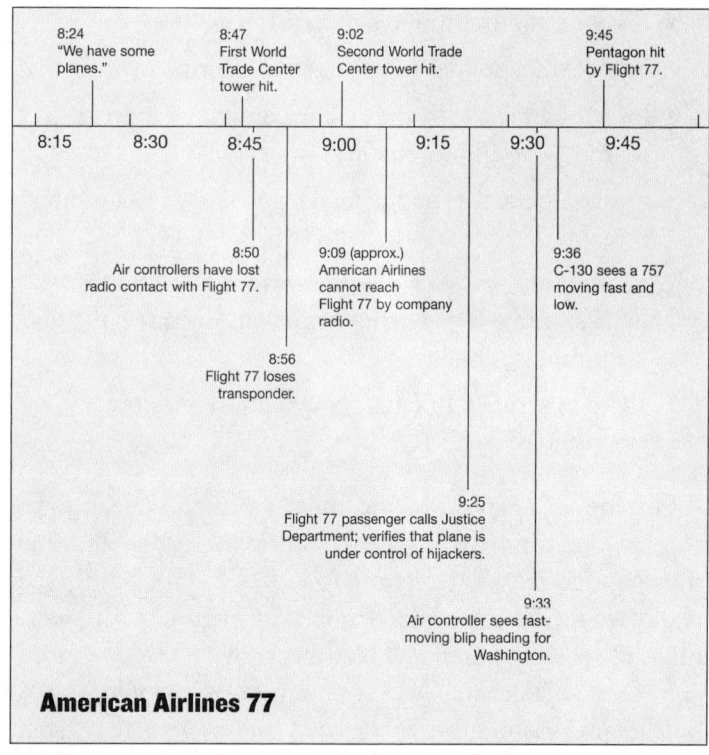

8:24	8:47	9:02		9:45
"We have some planes."	First World Trade Center tower hit.	Second World Trade Center tower hit.		Pentagon hit by Flight 77.

8:15   8:30   8:45   9:00   9:15   9:30   9:45

8:50
Air controllers have lost radio contact with Flight 77.

9:09 (approx.)
American Airlines cannot reach Flight 77 by company radio.

9:36
C-130 sees a 757 moving fast and low.

8:56
Flight 77 loses transponder.

9:25
Flight 77 passenger calls Justice Department; verifies that plane is under control of hijackers.

9:33
Air controller sees fast-moving blip heading for Washington.

American Airlines 77

license the centralization of injuring power rather than a decentralized and distributed authorization across the full citizenry that is, according to the U.S. Constitution, our legal right and our legal responsibility to protect. There is a second profound reason the act could not be (ought not to have been) carried out—the problem of consent, to which I will return when we come to United Flight 93.

Let us see what actions the military undertook during this time. The country has fourteen National Guard planes responsible for defending the country. Five of those planes —two F-15s from Otis Air Force Base on Cape Cod and three F-16s from Langley in Virginia—were called into action on September 11. These five planes were not the only military planes in the air that day. Once the Pentagon was hit, the FAA ordered all aircraft to land in a beautifully choreographed landing of 4,546 planes over a period of three hours. When the FAA announced the order, 206 military planes were in U.S. airspace (most engaged in routine exercises, actions unconnected to the immediate defense of the country); ninety remained in the air after the grounding (their duties have not been entered into the public record).[19] But it is only the five National Guard planes that were called into action against the seized passenger airliners that will be described here.

The two National Guard F-15s that took off from Otis Air Force Base on Cape Cod attempted to address the events taking place in New York City. They were called into action one minute before the first World Trade Center tower was hit; by the time the second tower was hit they were 71 miles—eight minutes—away from Manhattan. Should they then have continued down to the Washington area? (By this time, the plane destined for the Pentagon had its radio and transponder off and was reachable by neither air controllers nor the airline company.) The answer is no. The two F-15s needed to stay near New York City, where it was reasonable to worry that a third hijacked plane could approach. From September 11, 2001, until March 21, 2002, New York airspace was protected 24 hours a day by F-15s, F16s, and AWACS.

Three F-16s at Langley, Virginia, received their first order from Huntress Defense Section at 9:24 A.M. This is a late start: twenty-two minutes after the second World Trade Center tower has been hit, thirty-four minutes after the plane destined for the Pentagon has lost its radio, twenty-eight minutes after it has disappeared from secondary radar, and fifteen minutes after the airline company has failed to reach the plane on its own radio. By 9:30 A.M. the three Langley F-16s are in the air traveling at 600 mph toward New York City. Soon they are instructed to change their course and are told that Reagan National Airport is the target. They are flying at 25,000 feet.[20] The hijacked plane is flying at 7,000 feet. They reach Washington, D.C., at some unspecified time after the 9:45 collision of Flight 77 into the Pentagon. As they pass over the city, they are asked to look down and confirm that the Pentagon is on fire—confirmation that by this point civilians on the ground have already provided.

There are profoundly clear reasons why the military could not easily intercept the plane and bring it down in a rural area. But each of those reasons has counterparts in our longstanding military arrangements that should now be subjected to rigorous questioning. First: Flight 77's path was hard to track since its transponder had been turned off. Yes, that's true—and so, too, any missiles fired on the United States or its allies will surely be traveling without a transponder; their path will not be lucid; their tracking will not be easy. Second, the fact that Flight 77's radio was not working couldn't be taken as a decisive sign that it was a hijacked plane since at least eleven planes in the country had radios not working (nine of the eleven unconnected to the hijackings). Yes, that's true—and with missile defense there are likely to be not eleven but hundreds of decoys and false targets that will have to be nimbly sorted through. As difficult as it was to identify the third seized plane, it must be acknowledged that the flight had elements that made it far easier to identify than the enemy missiles our nation has spoken blithely about for decades: the direct voice confirmation provided by the passenger phone call to the Justice Department, most notably, will not have any counterpart on a missile attack; nor can we reasonably expect six layers of verification of any one enemy plane or missile.

A third crucial explanation for the failure to protect the Pentagon is that an F-16 cannot shoot down a passenger plane by arrogating to itself the right to decide whether the lives on board can be sacrificed to avert *the possibility* of even more lives being lost on the ground.[21] Yes, that is true —and yet for decades we have spoken about actions that directly imperil the full American citizenry (including presidential first use of nuclear weapons against a population that the president acting alone has decided is "the enemy") without ever obtaining the American citizenry's consent to those actions.

Each of these three explanations for why the attack on the Pentagon could not be easily averted raises key questions about our longstanding descriptions of the country's defense, and yet so far does not appear to have in any way altered those descriptions. September 11 has caused the United States and its allies to adjust their timetables only in those cases where the scenario imagined closely approximates the events that occurred in the terrorist attack itself. In England, for example, "MI5 has warned Ministers that a determined terrorist attempt to fly a jet into the Sellafield nuclear plant in Cumbria could not be prevented because it is only *two minutes'* flying time from transatlantic flight paths."[22]

While two minutes' time makes it impossible to defend Cumbria against terrorists, two minutes is apparently plenty of time for carrying out missile defense by the United States and NATO allies. Here is a post–September 11 description of England's "Joint Rapid Reaction Force": "A new satellite communications system has been installed to allow planners in Northwood to transmit target co-ordinates to the royal Navy's nuclear submarines equipped to fire Tomahawk cruise missiles. HMS *Trafalgar* and HMS *Triumph* in the Indian Ocean both have this system. *Within minutes* of the Prime Minister giving permission to fire from Downing Street, General Reith could pass on the orders to the submarine nominated to launch the precision attack."[23] What would be the response by Western democracies if a terrorist now used chemical, biological, or even nuclear weapons? In an article describing advice to Tony Blair from his defense ministers, we learn that "one of his most trusted advisers believes that a highly effective way of preventing such an attack is to threaten states that succor the terrorists with a nuclear wipe-out, *within minutes* of such an attack, without waiting for intelligence reports, United Nations resolutions or approval from NATO."[24] Does the Bush administration have plans in place for such attack? Might it be our duty to inquire?

The plane that took the Pentagon by surprise could not be stopped despite a *one hour and twenty-one-minute* warning that multiple planes had been hijacked, despite a *fifty-eight-minute* warning that the hijackers intended to maximize the number of casualties, despite a *fifty-five-minute* warning that Flight 77 might *possibly* be a hijacked flight, and despite a *twenty-minute* warning that Flight 77 was *certainly* a hijacked flight. Yet so confident are we of our ability to get information, of our power to decipher complex lines of responsibility, of the existence of evil and of the transparency of that evil, that we are still today talking about the two or three minutes to send cruise missiles and even nuclear genocide to foreign populations. This despite eleven months—475,000 minutes—in which we have been unable to determine who sent anthrax to the U.S. Senate and various centers of television communication.[25]

UNITED FLIGHT 93

United Airlines Flight 93 was a small piece of American territory—roughly 600 cubic meters in its overall size. It was lost to the country for approximately forty minutes when terrorists seized control. It was restored to the country when civilian passengers who became citizen-soldiers regained control of the ground—in the process losing their own lives.

The passengers on United Flight 93 were able to defend this ground for two reasons: first, they were able to identify the threat accurately because it was in their immediate sensory horizon (unlike the F-16s that hoped to intercept the plane that hit the Pentagon, the passengers on Flight 93 did not need to decipher their plane's flight path from the outside, nor make inferences and guesses about lost radio contact). The passengers were also able to get information from unimpeachable sources external to the plane: crucially, they did not rely on information from a single central authority but obtained it from a distributed array of sources, each independent of the others. Second, it was their own lives they were jeopardizing, their own lives over which they exercised authority and consent. On the twin bases of sentient knowledge and authorization, their collaborative work met the democratic standard of "informed consent."

When the U.S. Constitution was completed it had two provisions for ensuring that decisions about war-making were distributed rather than concentrated. The first was the provision for a congressional declaration of war—an open debate in both the House and the Senate involving what would today be 535 men and women. The second was a major clause of the Bill of Rights—the Second Amendment right to bear arms—which rejected a standing executive army (an army at the personal disposal of president or king) in favor of a militia, a citizen's army distributed across all ages, geography, and social class of men.[26] Democracy, it was argued, was impossible without a distributed militia: self-governance was perceived to be logically impossible without self-defense (exactly *what* do you "self-govern" if you have ceded the governing of your own body and life to someone else?).

United Flight 93 was like a small legislative assembly or town meeting. Figure 2 shows the assembly structure. The residents on that ground conferred with one another, as well as with people not residing on the plane. Records from the on-board telephones show that twenty-four phone calls were made between 9:31 A.M. and 9:54 A.M.; additional calls were made from cell phones.[27] In approximately *twenty-three minutes,* the passengers were able collectively to move through the following sequence of steps:[28]

1. *Identify the location throughout the plane of all hijackers and how many people each is holding.* We know that passengers registered this information in detail because they voiced the information to people beyond the plane: Todd Beamer relayed the information to Lisa Jefferson (a Verizon customer-service operator); Jeremy Glick relayed it to his wife;[29] Sandy Bradshaw to her husband; Mark Bing-

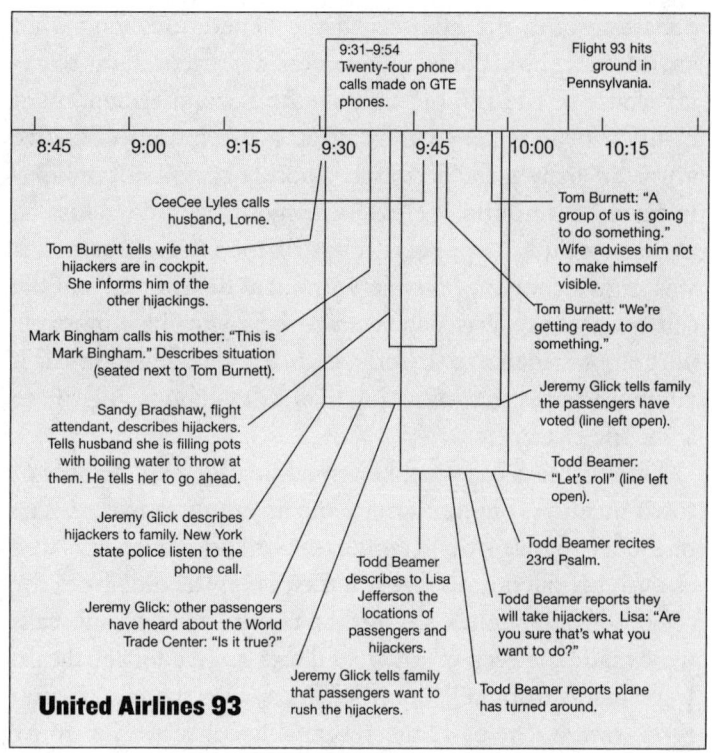

United Airlines 93

ham to his mother; Marion Britton to a close friend; Elizabeth Wainio to her stepmother; and CeeCee Lyles to her husband.

In terms of democratic self-defense, these conversations are crucial (both at step one and at each of the seven steps listed below) to preserving the civil frame that the founders identified as so essential to military defense. The conversations enabled extraordinary events to be tested against the norms of everyday life. They were both intimate and an act of record-making: how else to explain Mark Bingham's self-identification to his mother, "This is Mark Bingham." He both gave his mother the statement that the plane had been seized by hijackers ("You believe me, don't you?") and in effect notarized the statement by giving a verbal signature.

2. *Hear from sources outside the plane the story of World Trade Center towers.* This information was key: it informed the passengers that they would almost certainly not be making a safe landing; it also informed them that many people on the ground would also suffer death or injury from their plane.

3. *Verify by multiple sources outside the plane the World Trade Center story.* Jeremy Glick, for example, told his wife that the account of the World Trade Center attacks was circulating among the passengers. He explicitly asked her to confirm or to deny its truth: "Is it true?"

4. *Consult with each other and with friends outside the plane about the appropriate action.* Jeremy Glick told his family the passengers were developing a plan "to rush" the hijackers and he asked their advice. Todd Beamer told Lisa Jefferson the passengers will "take" the terrorists (she cautioned: "Are you sure that's what you want to do?"). Tom Burnett told his wife a group of us "is going to do something" (she urged him to lay low and not make himself visible). Sandy Bradshaw told her husband she was at that moment filling coffee pots with boiling water which she planned to throw at the hi-

jackers; she asked if he had a better plan (he tells her she has the best plan and to go ahead).

5. *Take a vote.* Jeremy Glick described the voting process to his wife as it was under way.

6. *Prepare themselves for taking a dire action that may result in death.* CeeCee Lyles, unable to reach her husband, left on the phone a recording of herself praying, then later reached him and prayed with him; Tom Burnett asked his wife to pray while he and others on the plane acted; Todd Beamer and Lisa Jefferson together recited the Twenty-third Psalm.

7. *Take leave of people they love.* Each of the passengers who was in conversation with a family member stated aloud his or her love for the listener; Todd Beamer asked Lisa Jefferson to convey his love to his family. The family members reciprocated: "I've got my arms around you," Elizabeth Wainio's stepmother told her.

8. *Act.*

Many passengers described the plan to enter the cockpit by force. Not every passenger assumed death was certain. Jeremy Glick left his phone off the hook, telling his wife, "Hold the phone. I'll be back." Todd Beamer also left the phone line open—either because he expected to come back, or as an act of public record-keeping. The two open lines permitted members of the Glick household and Lisa Jefferson to overhear the cries and shouts that followed, indicating that action was being taken. CeeCee Lyles, still on the phone with her husband, cried, "They're doing it!

They're doing it!" Confirmation is also provided by Sandy Bradshaw's sudden final words to her husband: "Everyone's running to first class. I've got to go. Bye."[30]

The passengers on United Flight 93 could act with speed because they resided on the ground that needed to be defended. Equally important, they could make the choice—formalized in their public act of an open vote—between certain doom and uncertain (but possibly more widespread) doom. They could have hoped that the hijackers would change their planned course; they could have known that death by either avenue was certain, but one avenue would take them to their deaths in several minutes (rushing the hijackers and crashing the plane) and the other avenue would perhaps give them another half-hour or hour of life (waiting for the plane to reach its final target). They could have chosen the second; many people have chosen a delayed death when given the same choice. It is, in any event, the right of the people who themselves are going to die to make the decision, not the right of pilots in an F-16 or the person giving orders to the person in the F-16—as both civilian and military leaders have repeatedly acknowledged since September 11.

It may be worth taking note of the fact that the hijackers themselves correctly foresaw that the threat to their mission would come from the passengers ("citizen soldiers") and not from a military source external to the plane. The terrorists left behind them multiple copies of a manual, five pages in

Arabic.[31] The manual is a detailed set of instructions for the hours before and after boarding the plane—"an exacting guide for achieving the unity of body and spirit necessary for success." The ritualized set of steps includes: taking a mutual pledge to die; carrying out a ritual act of washing, invocation, and prayer; and dressing according to prescribed recommendations on the tightness or looseness of clothing.

The manual does not tell the terrorists what to do if an F-15 or F-16 approaches the planes they have seized.[32] It instead gives elaborate instruction on what to do if passengers offer resistance. We should not ordinarily let ourselves be schooled by terrorists. But terrorists who seek to carry out a mission successfully have to know what the greatest threat to their mission is—and the handbook indicates that the great obstacles were perceived to be first, the passengers, and second, the reluctance the hijackers might feel to kill any resisting passengers. They are instructed at length and in elaborate detail to kill any resister and to regard the killing as "a sacred drama," a death carried out to honor their parents. (That the hijackers would unblinkingly crash into a skyscraper, taking thousands of lives, yet balk at the idea of killing people hand-to-hand and therefore require detailed counseling to get through it is perhaps no more surprising than the fact that we listen every day to casualty rates brought about by the military yet would not keenly kill in hand-to-hand combat.)

CONCLUSION

I have intended here to open a conversation about our general capacity for self-defense. I have compared the fate of the plane that hit the Pentagon and the plane that crashed in Pennsylvania. The military was unable to thwart the action of Flight 77 despite fifty-five minutes in which clear evidence existed that the plane might be held by terrorists, and despite twenty minutes in which clear evidence existed that the plane was certainly held by terrorists. In the same amount of time—twenty-three minutes—the passengers of Flight 93 were able to gather information, deliberate, vote, and act.[33]

September 11 involved a partial failure of defense. If ever a country has been warned that its arrangements for defense are defective, the United States has been warned. Standing quietly by while our leaders build more weapons of mass destruction and bypass more rules and more laws (and more citizens) simply continues the unconstitutional and—as we have recently learned—ineffective direction we have passively tolerated for fifty years. We share a responsibility to deliberate about these questions, as surely as the passengers on Flight 93 shared a responsibility to deliberate about how to act. The failures of our current defense arrangements put an obligation on all of us to review the arrangements we have made for protecting the country. "All of us" means "all of us who reside in the country," not "all of us who work at the Pentagon" or "all of us who convene when there is a meeting of the Joint Chiefs of Staff." What the Chiefs of Staff think, or what analysts at the Pentagon think, is of great interest (as are the judgments of men and women who by other avenues of expertise have thoughtful and knowledgeable assessments of security issues); it would be a benefit to the country if such people would now begin to share those views with the public. But such views can in no way preempt or abridge our own obligation to review matters, since the protection of the country falls to everyone whose country it is.

More particularly, September 11 called into question a key argument that has been used to legitimate the gradual shift from an egalitarian, all-citizens' military to one that is external to—independent of—civilian control: the argument from speed. The egalitarian model turned out to have the advantage of swiftness, as well as obvious ethical advantages. This outcome has implications for three spheres of defense.

1. *Defense against aerial terrorism.* To date, the egalitarian model of defense is the only one that has worked against aerial terrorism. It worked on September 11 when passengers brought down the plane in Pennsylvania. It again worked on December 22, 2001, when passengers and crew on an American Airlines flight from Paris to Miami prevented a terrorist (now called "the shoe bomber") from blowing up the plane with plastic explosives and killing 197 people on board. Two Air Force F-15s escorted the plane to

Boston and, once the plane landed, FBI officials hurried aboard; but the danger itself was averted not by the fighter jets or the FBI but by men and women inside the plane who restrained the six-foot-four-inch man using his own hair, leather belts, earphone wires, and sedatives injected by two physicians on board.

When a passenger plane is seized by a terrorist, defense from *the outside* (by a fighter jet, for example) appears to be structurally implausible from the perspective of time, and structurally impossible from the perspective of consent. The problem of time—time to identify that a plane has been seized, time to identify accurately which plane it is, time to arrive in the airspace near the seized plane—was dramatically visible in the case of the plane that hit the Pentagon, even though much more time and more layers of verification were available that day than are likely to be available in any future instance. The time difficulty was visible again on January 5, 2002, when a fifteen-year-old boy took off without authorization from Petersburg-Clearwater International Airport, crossed through the airspace of MacDill Air Force Base (the headquarters for the U.S. war in Afghanistan), and then flew into a forty-two-story Bank of America skyscraper in Tampa, hitting at the twenty-eighth floor. Two F-15 fighter jets "screamed" toward him from the south, but reached him only after he had completed his twenty-five-minute flight.[34] The time problem was visible once more on June 19, 2002, when a pilot and passenger in a Cessna 182 accidentally crossed into forbidden Washington Monument airspace, flew there for twelve miles (coming within four miles of the White House), and then crossed out again before armed F-16s from Andrews Air Force Base could reach them.

Even if the nearly insurmountable problems of time and perfect knowledge can one day be solved, how can the problem of consent be solved? There is no case in war where a soldier is authorized to kill two hundred fellow soldiers; how can an airman be authorized to kill two hundred fellow citizens? How can anyone other than the passengers themselves take their lives in order to save some number of the rest of us on the ground? During the seven months that F-15s and F-16s, armed with air-to-air missiles, flew round the clock over New York and Washington, what instructions did they have in the event that a passenger plane was seized? What instructions do they now have for their more intermittent flights?[35] Are such instructions something only high-ranking officials should be privy to, or might this be something that should be candidly discussed in public?

It seems reasonable to conclude that on September 11 the Pentagon could have been defended in one way and one way only, by the passengers on the American Airlines flight. This would have required three steps: that multiple passengers on the plane be informed about the World Trade Center towers;[36] that the passengers decide to act or instead to abstain from acting; and that, in the event that they choose to act, they be numerous enough to successfully carry out their plan. As far as we know, none of these steps took place—in part because, as far as we know, there were not multiple passengers on board who knew about the World Trade Center towers. It is possible that one or more of these steps took place, even though they have not been recorded.

In stating that the egalitarian model is our best and only defense against aerial terrorism, I do not mean that passengers in any one case *must* choose to act, or that—having so chosen—they will be successful. I mean only that this is the one form of defense available to us as a country, which passengers are at liberty to exercise or refrain from exercising. Measures taken by the nation that are internal to the plane (locks on cockpit door, the presence of air marshals, the cessation of the round-the-clock fighter jets over New York and Washington[37]) are compatible with this form of defense.

2. *National defense in the immediate present.* The contrast between the plane that hit the Pentagon and the plane that crashed in Pennsylvania invites consideration of the need to return to an egalitarian and democratic military not only in the specific case of aerial terrorism but in all measures we take for the nation's defense in the present year. Some may argue that we cannot generalize from one day. Can we generalize from zero days? One day is what we have. What makes this non-risky is that rather than requiring us to come up with some new system of government, all it requires is returning to, and honoring, the framework of our own laws.

Since September 11 we have witnessed many actions taken in the name of homeland defense that are indepen-

dent of, or external to, civilian control. Foreign residents
have been seized and placed in circumstances that violate
our most basic laws; the war against Afghanistan was under
way before we had even been given much explanation of its
connection to the terrorists, who were all from Saudi Arabia
or Lebanon or Egypt or the United Arab Emirates and not
from Afghanistan; that war now seems to be over even
though we don't know whether we eliminated the small circle around Osama bin Laden, for whose sake we believed we
were there; we are now tripping rapidly ahead to the next
war, listening passively to weekly announcements about an
approaching war with Iraq that has no visible connection to
the events of September 11; the president's formulation of
this future war sometimes seems to include (or at least not to
exclude) the use of nuclear weapons and the animation of
our nuclear first-use policy.[38] The decoupling of all defense
from the population itself lurches between large outcomes
(presidential declaration of war) and the texture of everyday life. According to the former chairman of the Federal
Communications Commission, the federal agency called
the National Communications Systems has "proposed that
government officials be able to take over the wireless net-
works used by cellular telephones in the event of an emergency," thereby pre-empting the very form of defense that
did work (the citizenry) and giving their tools to the form of
defense that did not work (the official government).[39]

We are defending the country by ceding our own powers
of self-defense to a set of managers external to ourselves.

But can these powers be ceded without relinquishing the very destination toward which we were traveling together, as surely as if our ship had been seized? The destination for which we purchased tickets was a country where no one was arrested without their names being made public, a country that did not carry out wars without the authorization of Congress (and the widespread debate among the population that such a congressional declaration necessitates), a country that does not threaten to use weapons of mass destruction. Why are we sitting quietly in our seats?

In the short run, returning to an egalitarian model of defense means: no war with Iraq unless it has been authorized by Congress and the citizenry; no abridgment of civil liberties; no elimination of the tools that enable citizens to protect themselves and one another (such as cell phones)—and above all, no contemplated use of nuclear weapons.

3. *National defense in the long run.* Europeans often refer to nuclear weapons as "monarchic weapons" precisely because they are wholly external to any powers of consent or dissent exercised by the population. In the long run, the return to an egalitarian model of national defense will require the return to a military that uses only conventional weapons. This will involve a tremendous cost: it will almost certainly, for example, mean the return of a draft. But a draft means that a president cannot carry out a war without going through the citizenry, and going through the citizenry means that the arguments for going to war get tested tens of thousands of times before the killing starts.

Our nuclear weapons are the largest arsenal of genocidal weapons anywhere on earth. These weapons, even when not in use, deliver a death blow to our democracy.[40] But even if we are willing to give up democracy to keep ourselves safe, on what basis have we come to believe that they keep us safe? Their speed? A Cessna plane (of the kind that proved impossible to intercept in Florida and Washington) travels at approximately 136 feet per second; a Boeing 757 (of the kind that proved impossible to intercept as it approached the Pentagon) travels at 684 feet per second; a missile travels at 6,400 feet per second.[41] On what have we based our confidence about intercepting incoming missiles, since the problem of deciphering information and decoupling it from false decoys will (along with speed) be much higher in the case of the missile than in the cases of the planes?[42]

Nuclear weapons are an extreme form of aerial terrorism. It is with good reason that we have worked to prevent the proliferation throughout the world of nuclear weapons (as well as biological and chemical weapons of mass destruction). But in the long run other countries of the world will only agree to abstain from acquiring them, or to give them up in cases where they already have them, when and if the United States agrees to give them up. The process of persuading Iraq, China, North Korea, India, Pakistan, as well as our immediate allies, to give them up will commence on the day we agree to restore within our own country a democratic form of self-defense.

2

TOO UTOPIAN?

RICHARD FALK

Ever since reading *The Body in Pain,* I have cherished the thought and insight of Elaine Scarry, that rarity among intellectuals, a truly original mind focused on the most fundamental civilizational challenges. Regardless of the theme, Scarry never is content with merely reproducing or even varying familiar ideas. Her consistently radical way of posing essential questions redirects inquiry in the most valuable ways and is a tribute to her disciplined and erudite imagination, which is put almost exclusively at the service of democratic citizenship in America. If I understand her correctly, the unifying *political* project that dominates Scarry's concerns is the redemption of citizenship and restoration of constitutionalism, especially given the subversive implications of current technology and strategic doctrines of destruction epitomized by nuclear weaponry. As with several other intriguing radicalisms, Scarry's argument recommends a return to principled conservatism.

To perceive the significance of September 11 in this light is Scarry's most daring undertaking of all, especially impressive because it cuts against the grain of pervasive intellectual tumult and confusion that has been our national lot for this past year. To what seems like the most important conversation in the history of this country, at least since the rise of Hitler, Scarry brings an illuminating clarity as she considers how we might reduce our vulnerability without deforming our constitutional democracy. To so help us understand this gruesome and unprecedented happening and the lessons it contains for how we defend ourselves—as individuals, as a society, and as a world—in the face of a mega-terrorist threat is both a heroic and a necessary undertaking. We can only give thanks that the republic contains a thinker of Scarry's quality and profundity, someone who focuses her energies so that we might discover how to act as vigilant citizens in this profoundly demanding situation.

Already in *The Body in Pain* Scarry recognized that nuclear weaponry has transformed war because of its omnicidal potential, but also because the government using such weapons, despite their magnitude, cannot pause to obtain meaningful consent even from citizens and their elected representatives at home, much less from people elsewhere affected so irretrievably by secret decisions here.

This observation now illuminates America's vulnerability to the September 11 attack, despite its insistence on a defense structure premised on the *speed* of response in the event of attack. The logic of the government's argument that there is no time to obtain a congressional declaration of war in such emergency circumstances, and the authority to use nuclear weapons, must thus be put "at the personal disposal" of the president. The further implication, underscored by Scarry, is that because the Constitution is suspended for this kind of ultimate decision, it seems fatuous to insist on congressional participation in lesser decisions, including conventional warfare. Indeed, since World War II the country's war commitments have bypassed the constitutional arrangement of authority with awesome consistency. Scarry has observed that this failure to relate war-making to procedures of consent virtually eliminates the relevance of law and morality to this most critical of all national decisions and decisively undermines the democratic character of our governing process.

What Scarry shows so vividly is that the supposed functional justification for this suspension of the rights of citizens is itself based on a huge technophilic illusion. We are a civilization victimized by the modernist idea that every threatening technological innovation can only be neutralized by offsetting technological moves of even greater magnitude. Over time, this has raised the stakes of conflict until we reach the absolute ceiling of human survival with nuclear weaponry. Even here, qualifications must be made to calibrate correctly the scope of the problem. When it comes to human cloning, the established authorities, although floundering, willingly rely on normative criteria to limit permissible technological innovation.

In relation to war-making, Americans, as members of society and adherents of a system of governance, have lost their confidence in all that might eventually have made the country "a light unto the nations": morality, rule of law, constitutional government, an engaged citizenry, and humane governance. Of course, this heritage was never without serious blight, considering the dispossession of indigenous peoples, slavery, gender discrimination, and a host of other social injustices. Yet the point remains: there were grounds for *projecting* American exceptionalism as a *goal*, even if not as an attainment. Such claims depend on the future tense, a sense of trajectory toward a goal that seemed plausible in relation to race relations, the status of women, and sexuality. But now this national trajectory has altered sharply for the worse.

Extending Scarry's assessment somewhat beyond its explicit reach, al Qaeda's tactical brilliance can be seen in its realization that the technological sophistication of American "power" provided no defense against dedicated unarmed individuals willing to die to carry out their mission of destruction. *In this regard,* the suicidal hijackers resembled the passengers on Flight 93. Both were effective within the frame of their intentions, and both sacrificed their lives knowingly for a cause deemed greater than themselves: in one case as jihadists bent on terrorist destruction and in the other as citizen warriors defending their society against enemies. What both sides overlooked was the potency of defensive responses that went beyond the vulnerabilities of technology. The exploits of the passengers of Flight 93 foiled the hijackers' plans, premised on the vulnerability of sophisticated technology.

Scarry proceeds in her analysis of September 11 to insist that we are best off as a people and as a world if we in the

United States learn anew to rely on what she calls the "egalitarian model" of defense. This is a characteristically radical argument bolstered by practical considerations, although given the depth of our technological self-entrapment, a seemingly utopian and politically unattainable position.

Still, the brilliance of Scarry's assessment of September 11 should not overwhelm our own capacity for interrogation. Three issues strike me as especially in need of further discussion.

First, Scarry provides no acknowledgement of the relevance of international law and the United Nations in her illustration of the application of the egalitarian model: "no war with Iraq unless it has been authorized by Congress and the citizenry." Because war affects people everywhere, it is only through respect for the limits imposed by international law that we can provide some assurance that the will of the powerful is not "the law" of world politics. In the case of Iraq, there is an almost total absence of international support for overlooking the U.N. Charter's prohibition on non-defensive force, and recourse to war would be a massive Nuremberg crime against the peace even if overwhelmingly authorized by Congress and the citizenry. One senses, at least implicitly, that Scarry's constitutional preoccupations may allow her to accept nationalist excesses provided they conform *procedurally* to the egalitarian model. Such an indulgence could be serious given the extent to which American political culture currently subscribes to a range of anti-egalitarian ideals, including militarist ambitions and an acceptance of technological determinism when it comes to war. In effect, the egalitarian model, as an inspiring and necessary utopia, must also be extended from sovereign state to the world when it comes to war-making.

Second, there is something of a disconnect in relation to war in the nuclear age. Strategists argue primarily about deterrence, not defense. They acknowledge the vulnerability of defense, at least provisionally, but then argue that defense is unnecessary because the attacker would be devastated automatically by a retaliatory strike, no matter how much harm its attack inflicted and how pointless retaliation might be. Now, with the Soviet Union out of the picture, strategists have qualified their argument and favor investing in defense so that America itself will not be deterred in its quest for global dominance. And further, because "rogue states" allegedly might pursue even a suicidal attack, a purely rational approach to security is somewhat obsolete. On this last point, the strategists *unreasonably* abandon deterrence so as to realize imperial dreams, for there is more reason to regard secondary states such as Iraq, Iran, and North Korea as deterrable powers than the former Soviet Union or present-day Russia and China. My point is that Scarry needs to meet this deterrence/defense cluster of positions to make her critical assessment truly responsive to the prevailing dialogue on these matters.

Third, Scarry does not address the problems of conflict with a megaterrorist adversary that cannot be definitively situated in space. What was the U.S. government to do on

September 12, other than attack Afghanistan? Could it be expected to sit back and wait for the next al Qaeda strike, perhaps even more devastating than the catastrophic harm visited on September 11? There was a plausible, although far from assured, connection between destroying the presumed nerve center of al Qaeda in Afghanistan and diminishing the challenge of megaterrorism. In contrast, no such connection exists with respect to Iraq. In fact, careful assessment shows that the megaterrorist threat is likely to be intensified by such an attack, creating a set of conditions where transfers of weapons of mass destruction to al Qaeda are most likely to occur. My point here is not mainly a substantive observation about weapons transfers. Instead, I want to emphasize that the template for defense and democracy associated with territorial warfare between sovereign states does not apply to the September 11 challenge. This would seem to validate weakening some of the constitutional constraints associated with fashioning an effective and legitimate response to a deeply concealed transnational terrorist network while reaffirming core commitments to law, morality, and constitutionalism. The burden of justification for the need for any abridgement of these commitments should be placed firmly on the government.

Sadly, this burden has not been assumed during the past year, resulting in gratuitous assaults on the liberties of citizens and the dignity of strangers and immigrants, especially from Islamic countries. I hope that Scarry will accept this distinction so as to make her egalitarian model a genuinely practical approach to national defense in the aftermath of September 11, while retaining the model's exhilarating and indispensable utopian qualities. We urgently need Elaine Scarry's empowering sense of post–September 11 patriotism. She tests our capacities and responsibilities as citizens, and she offers a scathing rebuttal to conventional wisdom on vital matters of war and peace.

DEMOCRACY WON'T HELP

PAUL W. KAHN

Sometimes democracy is not the answer. Though the experience of the passengers on Flight 93 was remarkable, it offers us little from which to generalize. There was no opportunity for democratic deliberation when Timothy McVeigh blew up the federal office building in Oklahoma, nor when anthrax was put in the mail. Terrorists have no particular reason to expose themselves to the risk of a small group's fury. For that reason, planes are unlikely to figure in future attacks—shipping containers, trucks, tunnels, bridges, microbes, chemicals, and nuclear wastes, maybe, but not commercial airliners. Indeed, after September 11, there may have been a real danger of mob action on airplanes. If you were of Middle Eastern descent and acted suspiciously, you were likely to find yourself targeted by passengers and crew.

Is there, nevertheless, a broader lesson to be learned about the role of democracy in deciding when and how to use American military power? Scarry reminds us that the power to declare war is constitutionally given to Congress. In her view presidential war-making is not only ineffective but illegal, yet there is little evidence that we can cure the deficiencies of our elected national officials with yet another appeal to the people. George Bush's ascension to office may have been exceptional, but his immense popular support in pursuit of the war on terror is not. The sad truth is that nationalism is easily triggered in support of wars, and even a president with no skills as a public speaker or a statesman can carry the country into war. The public turns against the use of force only when it fails. *That is the same moment at which they turn against politicians who have supported the use of force.* What is true of the people is even truer of Congress. Congress almost always has the power to stop the president from using force, regardless of the war-declaring power. The political reality is that it has no interest in doing so until popular sentiment has turned.

Pleas for a reinvigoration of Congress's war-declaring power are usually disguised pleas for a new American politics, one of mature deliberation among public-minded citizens who are willing to take a sober second look at their aroused passions. There is, however, no easy fix for a political body that is generally ignorant of the rest of the world, of recent history, and of the actual distribution of wealth and interests in its own country, while it relies on fewer and fewer media sources that themselves devote fewer and fewer resources to news coverage. No court can command Congress to exercise its responsibilities; no court can make the people deliberate. Generally speaking, we get the political leadership we deserve, and given the state of our national political knowledge, debate, and interests, we don't deserve much.

Appealing to eighteenth-century models to deal with twenty-first-century problems is unlikely to be successful. Scarry is right to point out that we have no adequate defense against many contemporary threats. Calling for popular armies and deliberation is not going to change this fact any more than spending a lot of money on high-tech weaponry. Vulnerability characterizes modern life. *Doing away with nuclear weapons, even if it were possible, is not going to change that.* One cannot do away with the knowledge that creation of weapons of mass destruction is possible. One cannot respond to the full range of motivations that individuals, groups, and nations have to create and deploy such weapons—at least if one wants to preserve a modicum of justice. The simple fact is that the very technology that makes modernity possible brings tremendous risks. Neither democracy nor justice can eliminate those risks.

To be concerned with democratic self-defense is an indulgence that may have tremendous costs to the rest of the world. The appropriateness of deploying American forces to secure others' well-being was a major policy issue before September 11, and it will remain regardless of whether or not we can defend ourselves from terrorist attacks. The character of a post–Cold War use of force showed itself in places like Bosnia, Rwanda, East Timor, and Kosovo. In each case, the question arose whether the West—and particularly the United States—would use force to stop massive human-rights abuses. In other words, would we risk our own forces for the defense of strangers?

When we are done hunting for Osama bin Laden, this question will remain. If one believes that prevention of such massive abuses is morally compelling, then appeals to democratic control in this country may not be helpful. Americans are isolationist in their policy preferences and lack the knowledge to have an informed opinion about the rest of the world. Before September 11, Americans would never have supported intervention in Afghanistan in order to save Afghan women from the abuses of the Taliban regime; but in the long run that may be our greatest contribution. *That issue was just as morally pressing before September 11, but it surely was not on our agenda.*

If we are concerned with deploying the immense military power of the United States for good in the world as we confront the twenty-first century, then we need to appreciate opportunities for presidential leadership. More than Congress and more than the public, the president is subject to the demands of international organizations and the pressures brought to bear by civic and political leaders from around the world. If we want the United States to stop genocide in places like Rwanda, we need to reject arguments that every risky deployment of U.S. forces requires a congressional declaration of war and advance democratic approval. We should do all that we can to encourage international policing, military deterrence, and the threat of real intervention against those who would commit mass atrocities. We should encourage U.S. participation in such deployments of force. The Constitution was not designed for such a task, nor is Congress likely to assume it. Intervention is, however, demanded of the United States by much of the world. They are right to make this demand, and I do not believe that the structure of the Constitution undermines the morally compelling response.

A POLICY FAILURE?

STEPHEN M. WALT

Elaine Scarry's "Who Defended the Country?" is an evocative metaphor masquerading as policy analysis. In this metaphor, two doomed planes symbolize contrasting approaches to national defense. Flight 77—the plane that struck the Pentagon—is used to illustrate the inadequacies of a hierarchical, technological approach to defense policy that is obsessed with speed. In contrast, Flight 93—which crashed in Pennsylvania after the passengers fought back —represents an approach to national defense that Scarry believes is both more effective and more consistent with American values.

Scarry and I probably agree on a number of specific policy issues, such as the folly of national missile defense or the need to preserve civil liberties in the wake of September 11. Unfortunately, her "analysis" tells us very little about the actual content of U.S. defense policy or the proper policies we should adopt in the future. Although her narrative is energetic and arresting, readers who do not share her views are unlikely to be persuaded. Even worse, those who may agree with her basic position won't find much additional support for their views.

How Good (or Bad) Is U.S. Defense Policy?

The main flaw in Scarry's article is her attempt to challenge the entire thrust of U.S. defense policy on the basis of a single set of events. Even if one grants that "the Pentagon could not defend the Pentagon" on September 11, it does not follow that our basic approach to national security is misguided. No complex organization can boast a 100 percent success rate, especially when it faces adversaries who are actively trying to outwit it. A proper evaluation of U.S. national security policy requires that we look at a broad sample of successes and failures while simultaneously taking into account events (both good and bad) that might have occurred but didn't. Scarry claims that "one day is all we have," but it would be silly to base our entire defense policy on the "lessons" of a single tragic morning. Focusing solely on a vivid and dramatic failure stacks the deck in favor of the critics, but it doesn't tell us what we are doing right and what we might be doing wrong.

What does the overall record look like? The United States has made many mistakes in its foreign and defense policy in Vietnam, the Middle East, Latin America, and elsewhere, errors that squandered billions of dollars and cost thousands of lives. These failures are balanced, however, by many successes: the postwar reconstruction of Europe and Japan, the creation of durable institutions for managing the world economy, the containment of Soviet expansion and eventual collapse of communism without a great power war, and the steady advance of democracy and human rights worldwide. U.S. foreign and defense policy may not deserve all the credit for these things, but it surely played a role. Similarly, at the very moment that Flight 77 struck the Pentagon, U.S. military forces were also deterring conflict on the Korean Peninsula, reassuring numerous allies in Europe and Asia, keeping the peace in Bosnia and Kosovo, and helping stabilize the simmering dispute between India and Pakistan. Perhaps these policies are all unnecessary, and maybe the United States (and the world) would be better off if the United States retreated to isolationism and left the rest of the world to its fate. But the metaphor upon which Scarry relies does not help us engage these issues.

Scarry's discussion of "speed" betrays a similar unfamiliarity with the underlying principles of U.S. defense strategy and the historical record of U.S. decision-making. In general, the emphasis on rapid responses has been confined to two basic situations. The first is conventional warfare, where the ability to respond quickly to changing battlefield conditions is an obvious advantage. The second situation is the fear of a "decapitation" strike. In this scenario, U.S. defense planners worried that a nuclear-armed adversary might try to avoid nuclear retaliation by launching a sneak attack against U.S. leaders and command and control capabilities. The danger of this sort of attack was remote, but demonstrating that U.S. forces could respond very rapidly made it even less likely.

If one looks at the historical record, moreover, rapid responses have been the exception rather than the rule. President Truman did not intervene the day the Korean War broke out, and U.S. entry into the Vietnam War occurred gradually, over the course of a decade, and enjoyed both popular and congressional support. The decision to reverse Iraq's invasion of Kuwait in 1990 was debated for weeks, and our interventions in Bosnia and Kosovo followed months or years of agonized introspection. Even the infamous Cuban Missile Crisis lasted nearly two weeks, and Kennedy and his advisors debated options extensively before settling upon a course of action. Although presidential administrations sometimes cite the need to respond rapidly in order to maximize their political autonomy, the historical record offers little evidence of a "hairtrigger" mentality.

Moreover, it is not clear what policy conclusions we should draw from Scarry's detailed deconstruction of the September 11 timetables. She criticizes the Defense Department's emphasis on speed, but her narrative shows that part of the problem on September 11 was our inability to act fast enough once warning was available. This failure occurred in part because the United States stopped spending much money on continental air defense once nuclear weapons were placed on missiles, a decision that has saved the United States hundreds of billions of dollars over the past four decades. But what lesson, then, should we draw from all this? Was the Pentagon struck because we have placed too much emphasis on "speed," or because we did not emphasize it enough?

How Should National Security Decisions Be Made?

Scarry's own preferred model of national security decision-making—as symbolized by the improvised "town meeting" on Flight 93—suggests that we should encourage direct citizen participation in key national security decisions. That is a laudable goal, but there is a big difference between public engagement, direct participation, and democratic accountability. In a republic of 285 million people, we cannot base every public-policy decision on face-to-face public deliberation or even some form of plebiscite. Instead, we sanction leaders who do not perform well (i.e., by voting them out of office) and we require key decisions to conform to constitutional principles and legislative approval. These institutions do not always work as well as we might wish, but Scarry does not offer any evidence to show that our existing political mechanisms have failed to produce an intelligent national security policy. Once again, accomplishing that task would require looking beyond September 11 and require her to provide a more comprehensive assessment of successes and failures.

There are at least two further problems with the model for decision-making that Scarry endorses. First, the "town meeting" model would be inappropriate in the face of an imminent attack. What if the president received intelligence of an imminent terrorist attack on the United States, possibly involving a nuclear, chemical, or biological weapon, and what if there was a good chance the attack could be thwarted by sending U.S. forces to destroy the weapon(s) in question? A rapid (and secret) response would be essential, and a public debate would simply tip off the adversary. It is worth noting that the passengers on Flight 93 did not "debate" their actions *openly:* they discussed options *covertly* so as not to alert the hijackers as to their intentions. The democratic safeguard in this scenario is not a public debate about how to respond; it is the capacity of the electorate to oust a leader whose judgment proves unreliable.

Second, Flight 93 is not a useful metaphor for the conduct of national security policy precisely because these individuals were forced to act in isolation from the normal constraints that govern policymaking in a democracy. Do we really want any group of Americans who believe they are in imminent danger to be empowered to use force to defend themselves, provided that they have "deliberated" or "voted" in some fashion? Of course not. Democracy is a wonderful thing, but lynch mobs can vote, too. The passengers on Flight 93 are regarded as heroes because they responded bravely to what we now *know* was a genuine danger, but we hardly want to enshrine this type of independent action as the ideal response whenever someone feels threatened. At the national level we want national security decisions to be conducted by officials who are both empowered and held accountable by the electoral process and whose conduct is constrained by laws and constitutional principles.

Finally, Scarry's near-exclusive focus on the two planes

diverts her from the more important lesson from September 11, one that should be central to her concern for democratic control of U.S. policy. September 11 shows that the United States cannot be engaged in every corner of the world without provoking considerable resentment. Over the past decade, the United States has taken on a more active military role in the Islamic and Arab worlds—and especially the Persian Gulf—while maintaining its one-sided support for Israel. It has also stuck its nose in lots of other countries' business, showing scant regard for global opinion while doing so. These policies do not justify what al Qaeda did, of course, but Americans should hardly be surprised when its efforts to mold world politics trigger resentment and retaliation. And what has been missing is any serious national debate about America's global military presence: should the United States be the world's gendarme or not? When and where should we use force, and when should we stay out? By focusing solely on a single morning and on the fate of two doomed planes, Scarry's article—ambitous though it is—fails to come to grips with that fundamental question.

Thus, my main reaction to "Who Defended the Country?" is disappointment. Professor Scarry has provided a vivid narrative, but her timetables, analogies, and breathless rhetoric do not tell us very much about how we should deal with these problems in the future. And because I suspect we would agree on a number of contemporary security issues, I wish her article made a better case.

A SUCCESS OF DEMOCRACY?

CHARLES KNIGHT

I share many of Elaine Scarry's concerns about the direction of American national defense. Over the last fifty years, and especially after conscription ended in the 1970s, our national defense has become the domain of professionals, increasingly right-wing in their political perspectives, increasingly removed from the citizens they serve, and increasingly operating outside of meaningful democratic oversight and control. In the Bush administration, radical neoconservatives hold key positions of influence, and after September 11 they have been emboldened to talk openly about a new American empire and the need to build up and reform the armed services better to serve as its shock troops and gendarmes.

During the past year, Congress has shown little inclination to engage the enormous strategic questions raised by the administration's "war on terrorism" and has mostly restricted its participation to quick approvals of large funding increases for the Pentagon and other executive security agencies. Now the administration is leading the country into a preventive war against Iraq. If Congress's recent timidity and passivity is any guide to future behavior, they will go through the motions of debate and give the president the broad "resolution of war" that he wants to go after Saddam Hussein. Realistically, the current Congress is just too conservative to mount any serious challenge to a president's will to war.

While many of Elaine Scarry's concerns are right on the money, the story she tells of 9/11 to support her case has numerous problems. I will focus here on three issues.

First, Scarry's initial assertion that "the difficulty of defense on September 11 turned in large part on the pace of events" is overstated. The central problem that day was *strategic surprise*—specifically, no responsible official seemed to have understood that commercial airliners could be turned into powerful weapons by determined enemies. In comparison, it would have taken a squadron of fighter-bombers to take down the twin towers. The danger from fighter-bombers is well understood, and the United States has air defenses ready to take down attacking bombers; moreover, our own fighters and bombers are very well guarded on their bases. In contrast, our professional security forces completely missed the threat inherent in our large commercial airliners and had done nothing serious to defend their flight decks from hijackers.[1]

Speed is important to surprise. More important, though, are elements of invention and of deception, including long periods of quiet in which one's opponents may relax their vigilance. On September 11, the speed of the aircraft was less important than their vulnerability to hijacking and the explosive power of their large fuel tanks when flown into a building.

Scarry is also interested in speed in a normative sense. She cites the supposed exigencies of modern threats as "the most frequent argument used to excuse the setting aside of the Constitution." I agree in the sense that it is an "excuse" and not the truest reason. What we have witnessed in this country is a steady aggrandizement of the executive's national security power and prerogative since at least the beginning of the Cold War, with only a brief interruption after the unsuccessful Vietnam War. I doubt, however, that lack of time for deliberation was very high among the reasons why Congress has yielded ground to the executive.

Second, Scarry's argument for a more egalitarian defense strategy falters as soon as she introduces her thesis that "a form of defense that is external to the ground that needs to be defended does not work as well as a form of defense that is internal to the ground that needs to be protected." She then examines in detail the story of the plane that hit the Pentagon (failed defense) and the plane that crashed in Pennsylvania ("successful").

She asks us to consider that "each of the two planes was a small piece of U.S. ground," but in that sense, neither defense was successful because both planes crashed, killing all on board. Only by defining success as having "disabled the hijackers' mission" can she construe the story of Flight 93 as a success. It is true that the downing of Flight 93 successfully aborted the hijackers' primary mission, and if we then consider the supposed target in Washington, D.C., as the ground to be defended, then whatever defense actions brought down Flight 93 were done external to the ground to be protected. The internal ground in this instance was the plane itself, and its protection failed.

In terms of Scarry's concept of internal and external defense, I see no difference whether Flight 93 crashed as a result of action by the passengers, by the hijackers, or by air defense interception. In all cases the action would be taken external to the ultimate ground to be defended.

Finally, Scarry builds her argument around what has come to be known as the "heroes' story" of Flight 93—the story that a group of passengers rushed the flight deck and brought the plane down. There is fairly good evidence that a group of passengers did try to rush the hijackers, but whether they succeeded in entering the flight deck and therein causing the crash is not known.

I am agnostic about the cause of the crash of Flight 93. The government had the intention and the capability to shoot down the plane, but whether the government did or not cannot yet be determined. Nevertheless, it is worth mentioning some facts that Scarry has wrong or has omitted:

- She says "the country has fourteen National Guard planes responsible for defending the country." There may have been only fourteen on "high alert" that morning, but the country also has many hundreds that can be quickly readied and scrambled in an emergency.

- Five high-alert planes were scrambled, but we also know of other lower-alert National Guard planes that scrambled from Toledo, not far from where Flight 93 turned back toward Washington, and from Syracuse.

- Confirming a shoot-down order that morning, Dan Balz and Bob Woodward tell this story in the *Washington Post:* "In the White House bunker, a military aide approached the Vice President. 'There is a plane eighty miles out,' he said. 'There is a fighter in the area. Should we engage?' 'Yes,' Cheney replied without hesitation." It is likely that a (classified) standing executive order exists that made this conversation superfluous. Nevertheless, the air defense operations officer might well have requested affirmation from the White House before the extraordinary act of shooting down a civilian airliner.

- Scarry mentions the speed of intercept planes only once, when she notes that they reportedly flew north from Langley at 600 mph in the minutes before the Pentagon crash. However, F-16s and F-15s are capable of flying at more than twice that speed, and a higher speed would allow enough time to intercept Flight 93 from either the East Coast or the near-Midwest.

Both the heroes' story and the shoot-down story are plausible, and it seems likely that if one hadn't happened the other would have. If the heroes' direct action resulted in the plane crashing, then it happened only moments before a National Guard plane would have shot it down. And if a fighter shot it down, it probably happened in the midst of the first stage of the heroes' action. We simply don't know which happened. In terms of evaluating defenses it doesn't matter very much. Either way Washington, D.C., was saved from further damage, and either way the plane crashed. The only difference, an important difference in terms of how the story plays as inspirational wartime lore, is that if the heroes acted first and if there was in fact no National Guard fighter in the area they would have had a chance to wrest control from the hijackers, signal ground control, and take the plane in for a safe landing. That would have been a far better ending to the story. (Readers can find an informative and fairly evenhanded, if not highly disciplined, Flight 93 Web site at www.flight93crash.com.)

AN INFORMED CITIZENRY

ANTONIA CHAYES

Elaine Scarry's provocative article illuminates the debate about what went wrong on September 11. Mesmerized by the power of technology, of which speed is one part, our defense establishment indeed was less than fully capable of adequate response. But terrorism has demonstrated even more serious shortcomings in government that may lead to policy choices quite different from those proposed by Scarry.

Civilian control of the military is not the major issue in dealing with terrorism's shadowy threat. We have civilian control: the problem is how that control is exercised. The Vietnam War, for example, was not dominated by military adventurism; the president held the reins of policy firmly in his hands and involved himself in minute operational details. Ultimately, the democratic process began to work as it should, and erosion of popular support and active protest brought the war to an end without victory. A democracy the size of the United States requires delegation to elected representatives. No national policy can be sustained by citizens at town meetings. But we as voters can voice our policy objections to our representatives.

The problem in responding to September 11 and addressing the threat of terrorism, in my view, is less the concentration of power that Scarry focuses on than the failure of the interest and alertness of voters to make demands on those we elect. Thus far, we have not had a widespread, lively debate on the strategy for a comprehensive defense against terrorism. Three major areas strike me as deserving intense public attention. The independent commission investigating 9/11 will certainly deal with some of them.

Failure to analyze intelligence. Much has already been written about the failures to act on available information. The CIA knew about the Malaysia meetings involving the hijacker Midhar. The NSA had information on the hijacker Hazmi. The joint congressional investigation has yielded more such shocking deficits of intelligence analysis.[1] Bureaucratic inertia, combined with excessive caution, explains many of the failures. Traditional bureaucratic jealousies may explain even more about the failure to piece together information held by a number of agencies but not shared among them. What has been aired in the press may only be the tip of the iceberg.

This is not a new problem. But one year after September 11, little reform has been accomplished, and few serious internal intelligence improvements have been made visible to the public. It is an art to piece together a picture from the millions of scraps of data that are available. American intelligence agencies are well funded, and the magnitude and complexity of the problem warrants better placed and more wisely used talent. Inattention to pieces of information that might be important to the security of the nation is intolerable.

Lack of policy focus. Closely related to the failure to analyze intelligence is the failure to plan a course of action that will deal more effectively with the problems uncovered. U.S. leadership had ample and specific warning of a sequence of escalating terrorist attacks. After the initial bombing of the World Trade Center in 1993, the U.S. embassies in Nairobi, Kenya, and Dar es Salaam, Tanzania, on August 7, 1998, and the USS *Cole* in Yemen, October 12, 2000, we should have been fully alerted to the scope and reach of al Qaeda and developed both short- and long-range plans to combat its threat. The problem was clearly more complex and nuanced than any immediate retaliation could solve. Certainly, the bombing of irrelevant sites in Sudan and Afghanistan at the end of the Clinton administration accomplished little. The swift attack on Afghanistan did succeed in destroying the Taliban's grip on Afghanistan and its harbor for training and incubating al Qaeda terrorists. But a comprehensive, long-range strategy of action will require deeper thought and wider popular discussion than we have had thus far.

For that reason, one can question not only a planned attack on Iraq, but the entire two-war scenario that has dominated our military planning since the end of the Cold War. We may have or can acquire the military power to deal with two major regional conflicts. But it is doubtful that the nation possesses the leadership power that can be devoted to two major politico-military strategies, especially when one must be addressed to such an elusive area as worldwide terrorism. The Bush administration argues that Saddam Hussein's regime is a potential terrorist threat, all the more so because it has used and is developing more weapons of mass destruction. But it has not made the case that full-scale military operations against Iraq can be accomplished while sufficient attention is paid to many other pockets of terrorism such as Indonesia, Egypt, Libya, Syria, and Saudi Arabia, where the strategy of the United States may be complicated by an Iraq war and require military, diplomatic, and economic efforts that require sustained attention from the highest levels.

The "war on terrorism" is likely to take a backseat to the war on Iraq, with dire consequences to American security. Where is public discussion? Fearing electoral repercussions, the opposition is afraid to question a president bound for war. The administration has diverted attention not only from the war on terrorism, but from alliance relationships and all other issues.

Arrogance and American exceptionalism. American military power may defeat Saddam Hussein. But alone, our power is not sufficient to combat terrorism. The administration asked for cooperation from nations all over the world in intelligence-sharing and finding and prosecuting terrorists in their midst. From the results of efforts by Great Britain, Pakistan, Germany, and Spain, among others, we found that international cooperation has been critical. The

9/11 terrorists used many nations for their conspiracy and preparation.

Despite the demonstrated need for help, we have managed to erode support from major allies such as Germany not only by our intention to attack Iraq in violation of our international obligations under the U.N. Charter, but in the constant assertion of "hard power" and indifference to other international legal concerns. For example, securing a Security Council resolution demanding intrusive, no-notice inspections is not only sound international law, it is sound international politics. It may be a necessary political prelude to international support for war and especially its aftermath. It takes time to make the case that Iraq is the paramount terrorist threat. Military sanctions for violating a strong Security Council resolution are very different from unilateral war. But arrogance may result in quick, unsanctioned action.

In the end, my policy prescription for "civilian control" is for an informed citizenry to act through the representative processes. We need to put some iron in the backs of our legislators to ask the tough questions and to insist on legal processes—internally and externally. An egalitarian citizen-military, in contrast, can too easily be turned into an armed militia that will shoot a Sikh gas station proprietor out of ignorance.

THE SLIDE INTO PASSIVITY

CATHERINE LUTZ

As people lay dying in Vietnamese villages and rice fields in 1970, town meetings about U.S. national defense were held in Rowan Park and at a GI coffeehouse in Fayetteville, North Carolina, as well as on post at nearby Fort Bragg. Some of the soldiers there had joined with civilians to collect information about the war, publish newspapers like the GI's *Bragg Briefs,* and make a public case that the war was not constitutional, ethical, or strategically sound.[1] Animated in some ways by the same sense of emergency as on Flight 93—lives were at stake with each passing minute—these public debates clearly represented highly democratic approaches to the question of war.

The debates occurred at a point in the evolution of U.S. military institutions and U.S. democracy that is important to reexamine in the light of Elaine Scarry's argument. With historical examples like this in mind, we can begin to answer the most provocative question she raises in her enlightening essay: "why are we sitting quietly in our seats" as our military institutions are hijacked to fundamentally fascist purposes and authoritarian means? Since the democratic renaissance in defense matters evident in 1970, there have been several changes that have encouraged this citizen passivity, including the end of conscription, the privatization of defense, media corporatization, and the redefinition of national defense as "U.S. security interests."

Many assume the military began its escape from civilian control with the 1973 shift to an all-volunteer force. But while today's volunteer army is more politically conservative than the civilian population or than past armies, it is not personal politics but the intersection of those politics with particular wars and home front experiences that helps determine how military institutions respond to civilian demands for openness. While the vigorous debate about the Vietnam War resulted from an army drafted into a highly immoral and unsuccessful war, many soldiers emerged from the conflict believing they had been betrayed by both civilian leadership and the media; they responded with more secrecy and a more dismissive attitude toward civilians.

Moreover, sustaining a huge volunteer force requires more compensation than a drafted army, both in terms of income and other benefits. The latter includes a kind of super-citizenship status delivered through recruitment ads and political rhetoric. Many civilians have been more than happy to give tax money, elevated social status, and institutional control to the military in exchange for not having to send their own children to war. Some civil and military leaders have argued for a return to the draft on fairness grounds, but they have underestimated the power of a conscripted army to demand far more of democracy than fairness and far less war as well.

Two other social changes have contributed to citizens' passivity toward the military, both of which have resulted in the militarization of the "civil frame" itself. The first is the privatization of defense through corporatization. Every day, such companies as Raytheon and Honeywell take in new employees from the Pentagon and in return sell it military goals, plans, and technologies in return. Glossy advertisements for the latest artillery products fill military professional journals, and these same military-industrial marketeers move freely between the highest levels of military corporations and the government. Vice President Dick Cheney famously went from the position of secretary of defense during the Gulf War to CEO of Halliburton— where he made $30 million in two years, with some of the company's new riches coming from U.S. Army contracts —to vice-commander-in-chief. Out of such a system has come little data for citizens to process and much personal enrichment, corruption, fraud, and waste. It has produced what Mary Kaldor calls the "baroque arsenal"[2] and U.S. leadership of the international arms trade and its attendant blowback.

Second, the corporatization of the media has limited the amount of information citizens have about the military. The new media megacompanies have downsized the number of journalists in the workforce, and they and their advertisers avoid biting the government hand that feeds them.[3] The dumbing-down process has only accelerated since September 11, as U.S. political leaders have used extensive airtime and a friendly news frame to declare that dissent or even discussion of defense policy options is treasonous.

Finally, since World War II, a more imperial concept of "national security" has replaced that of defense. The former notion can encompass more easily explicit U.S. political and economic goals around the globe. Moreover, security is defined as a singular, national matter, assumed to be equally available to all citizens. In fact, while war and military spending benefit many state and corporate elites, those at the other end of the widening wealth gap face a higher risk of early death due to violence or poor nutrition and health care.[4] The collective defense provided by international or transnational law barely enters the discussion in a field defined not only by the erosions of our democratic culture, but by the Constitution's framing in the language of the nation-state.

Elaine Scarry begins to imagine a radically different response to the violence in our midst. We must take her vision a step further and imagine a future that retrieves our institutions to wider public interest and control. We might then roll back the U.S. empire and focus instead on violence prevention, true intelligence, and strategies for policing rather than civilian-killing aerial bombardment. One hopes that most people would see these as more important and humane methods of protecting each other.

SADDAM AND DEMOCRACY

REAR ADMIRAL EUGENE J. CARROLL, JR.,
U.S. NAVY (RET.)

He may be Satan incarnate but Saddam Hussein appears to be doing a great service to American citizens by giving new life to the democratic process in America. As early as June of this year, President Bush and his closest advisors appeared committed to a preemptive war against Saddam's Iraq without seeking the approval of American citizens or the U.S. Congress. This arrogance has been suitably rewarded with a remarkable upsurge of public efforts questioning not only the wisdom of a war but also the constitutional authority of the president to initiate an attack on Iraq.

It is in this context that Elaine Scarry asks extremely important and timely questions about the role of citizens in defending our nation against violence in a world far different than the one known to the drafters of the U.S. Constitution. While she explores this theme through the failure of defense on September 11, her insight into the continuing importance of the Constitution's requirements for consent can be wisely applied as we anticipate our actions in Iraq. Scarry's call for a democratic form of self-defense provides an important springboard for a larger debate about national security and the citizenry's consent to the role of the U.S. military in the world today.

In truth, the democratic process has been badly short-circuited ever since September 11, 2001, when the president and his principal advisors committed the United States to a "war on terrorism." The rising level of resistance to the president and his bellicose advisors is all the more remarkable because our leaders have cast the war on terrorism in stark terms: either you are for them or you are against American security. Reasonable debate—the kind that Elaine Scarry invites—to consider alternatives to pre-emptive military action as the primary means of dealing with international terrorism has not been welcomed. Without challenge, the president has pursued a single-minded approach: the military budget for 2003 increased by $48 billion (up 14 percent) while no significant additions were made to funds for the State Department to pursue diplomatic initiatives or initiate helpful foreign aid programs.

Fortunately, debate eventually emerged despite this climate. Even Representative Dick Armey, the arch-conservative House Majority Leader, has urged caution, joined by former national security advisor General Brent Scowcroft; former U.S. ambassador to the United Nations Richard Holbrooke; and the former commander-in-chief of the U.S. Central Command, General Anthony Zinni. Vice President Dick Cheney's hawkish speech to a veterans' group in August—in which he categorically committed the

United States to depose Saddam Hussein through military action—has further stimulated political dissent both within the United States and from abroad.

We must trust the democratic process to determine the wisest course of action in this perilous situation. Americans (and the world community) need to ask why the United States considers it is justified to initiate hostilities against Iraq in blatant violation of Chapter VII of the U.N. Charter. How will deposing Saddam Hussein bring an end to international terrorism? Will Iran be next on the White House list? Or will it be Syria? Does the United States intend to exploit its superpower role everywhere by initiating preemptive military actions whenever we assert that a threat exists to America's security?

Elaine Scarry provides a road map for the debate by focusing on the need for citizen consent and questioning all uses of nuclear weapons; but it will also be critical to consider a number of practical alternatives to war, including diplomatic initiatives. The primary one is strong U.S. leadership in the U.N. Security Council to revitalize a comprehensive inspection regime in Iraq. As I write in mid-September, following the president's U.N. address, such action seems to be bearing fruit. But even if inspections fail due to Iraqi duplicity and obstruction, it will likely rally support for U.N. military action by demonstrating that Iraq is determined to hide unlawful efforts to develop weapons of mass destruction that threaten world peace.

Next, the debate must explore the linkage between the

putative Iraqi threat and resolution of the Israeli-Palestinian conflict. The administration argues that strong U.S. action against Iraq will demonstrate forceful U.S. leadership in the region and actually facilitate progress in resolving the Palestinian issue. Critics charge in reply that a war against Iraq will harden opposition among Islamic states and further radicalize terrorist elements in their intifada against Israel and the United States.

A number of other issues regarding the actual conduct of any war against Iraq lie within the jurisdiction of the Pentagon, where public participation is not possible or appropriate. Nevertheless, before we attack, the problems of a post-war occupation must be addressed openly and agreement reached that America is prepared to carry out the onerous task of maintaining order within Iraq and defending its territorial integrity after we have brought down Saddam Hussein. It will be a terrible irony if we "win the war" but "lose the peace" by a failure to defend the nation whose government we have just destroyed. Security and stability throughout the Middle East require the continued existence of Iraq within its present borders. If we unilaterally initiate the attack without U.N. authorization, former Secretary of the Navy and Vietnam veteran James Webb has asked if we would be willing to perform occupation duties for thirty years, or longer. He also noted that a continuing U.S. presence in Iraq might weaken our ability to control international terrorism in many other regions such as Africa, Asia, and South America.

In summary, critical questions need to be asked and answered before any decision concerning a war on Iraq can be made wisely. A searching debate in the best traditions of American democracy must lead to that decision. Saddam Hussein may be contributing to that debate unwittingly but, as a concerned and responsible citizen, Elaine Scarry may take great satisfaction in her valuable efforts to inform and stimulate American citizens to participate in that debate.

CITIZENS AND ARMS CONTROL

RANDALL FORSBERG

I heartily agree with Elaine Scarry that U.S. government decisions about the use of armed force, and particularly about the possible use of nuclear weapons, are not subject to anything near an adequate degree of democratic control or popular consent. I agree that even if nuclear weapons are not used, maintaining a nuclear arsenal is not compatible with democratic governance; and that the best hope for safety from a nuclear holocaust, both in this country and elsewhere, would be for the United States to take the lead in moving the world toward nuclear disarmament. Finally, I agree that if the United States took the lead in supporting global steps toward nuclear disarmament, other countries with nuclear weapons would be likely to follow.

But some of Scarry's other arguments are wrong or misleading. First, abolishing nuclear weapons would not require a return to the draft or a huge increase in U.S. conventional military forces. All such forces are intended for use in foreign wars because no country has the capability to launch a major conventional attack on U.S. territory. The existing U.S. army, navy, and air force are much larger than would be needed to deter or win any near-future threat of major war overseas (regardless of how one might view the merits of U.S. involvement in any such war). This would still be the case if nuclear weapons were abolished.[1]

Second, the speed of a possible U.S.-Russian or U.S.-Chinese exchange of nuclear-armed missiles—the thirty minutes it takes for a ballistic missile to go from one side of the world to the other—has not eliminated democratic control altogether. Members of Congress, representing their constituents, have an opportunity during budget season every year to insist that policies regarding the retention and possible use of nuclear weapons be changed radically. But there has never been a congressional attempt to require administration support for U.S. policies aimed at global nuclear disarmament.

Third, the United States does not need a civilian militia or universal military service in order for citizens to defend themselves in an egalitarian manner because, to a first approximation, there is nothing to defend against—that is, there is no conventional military threat to U.S. territory. The only threats of massive violence that face U.S. citizens are 1) the unpredictable, isolated attacks that might be undertaken by non-state terrorist or criminal groups; 2) more severe terrorist-type threats that could be posed by hostile governments with access to nuclear, chemical, or biological weapons; and 3) the longstanding, well-known danger of a Russian or Chinese nuclear missile attack. None of these threats can be diminished, deterred, or effectively defended against by a conventional military force, whether professional or draft, executive or egalitarian. Scarry argues that terrorist threats using commercial airliners can be eliminated by agreement among the passengers to sacrifice their own lives, if necessary, but it is hard to think of another type of threat in which ordinary citizens can foil an attack by voluntarily risking their own lives. If terrorists put some lethal substance in a city's water supply, for example, ordinary citizens would be hard put to save lives through self-sacrifice or any kind of voluntary individual action.

To some extent, these criticisms involve matters of detail. I agree on the more important points:

- U.S. citizens would be safer than they are now if nuclear weapons were abolished and their lives were no longer in the hands of politicians authorized to order the use of nuclear weapons on a few minutes' notice.
- The lack of democratic control over U.S. military policy is profound.

To these I would add one other key point: The lack of democratic control over U.S. military policy lies most profoundly in the lack of general knowledge that *none* of the Defense Department's spending goes to defend U.S. territory, in the narrow and strict sense of the term "defense." If we prorate infrastructure and overhead, 10 percent of U.S. military spending goes to nuclear deterrence, the dangerous policy that Scarry and I oppose; 90 percent goes to conventional forces intended for intervention abroad. To reestablish democratic control over military policy we would need not only to abolish nuclear weapons, but also to eliminate nearly all U.S. conventional forces—or else engage citizens in a vigorous, well-informed debate on policy issues and options in the areas of international affairs, foreign policy, and interventionary uses of armed force.

I am currently working on two popular campaigns focused on increasing citizen input in precisely these two areas. UrgentCall.org is an Internet-based grass-roots campaign that calls for the United States to build on decades of international nuclear arms control agreements and continue to move, step by verifiable step, toward global nuclear disarmament. Global Action to Prevent War (www.globalactionpw.org) is an international coalition-building program that combines steps to reduce the outbreak of armed conflict around the world with measures to reduce unilateral military intervention and instead strengthen reliance on collective security and the rule of law, as originally envisioned in the U.N. Charter.

After working in this field for more than three decades, I conclude that increasing citizen knowledge about and input into national military decisions is, not surprisingly, an incredibly difficult undertaking. By tradition, this field is left to experts, and that is likely to be the case until colleges offering liberal arts degrees require an introductory course in security policy. Yet democratic control in this area is essential to the full development and flowering of democratic institutions, and equally essential to the safety and well-being of ordinary citizens here and throughout the world.

THE REALITIES OF WAR

ELLEN WILLIS

Invoking the saga of Flight 93 as an exemplary alternative model to our top-down, technocratic, citizen-proof defense system, Elaine Scarry appeals to one of our more potent national myths: that the American democratic spirit calls forth an inventive pragmatism, a capacity for creative action that authoritarian systems and cultures lack. It's a myth that goes back to the revolution and the triumph of America's ragtag guerrillas against the rigid, hierarchical British army. What if anything does that myth tell us about our present situation? Are we still that country? Do we believe that democracy is not only morally right, or socially advanced, but practical? That it can serve us in the face of mortal danger?

These are uncomfortable questions. The project of a democratic defense is surely crucial to the democratic project in general, yet it is also in a way oxymoronic. In war or political violence, at least one party tries to coerce or dominate another; it is not played by democratic rules. What is the other party to do? If speed as an excuse for abrogating those rules does not hold up (and Scarry makes a convincing case that it does not), the "argument from secrecy"— equally familiar, equally anathema to an open, democratic society and equally misused—is harder to dispel. Surprise is a central element of war. We need to conceal from our enemies what we are doing, and at the same time to find out what they are doing; yet as soon as we accept any form of censorship or spying, it becomes difficult if not impossible adequately to assess what is being kept secret and whether it really needs to be. And what of the most obvious form of popular defense, a citizen army? In practical terms that means a draft, for most people will not volunteer to fight if they can't count on everyone else to do so. In my view, a draft (including women as well as men) would be more democratic than our present careerist model of military service, which not only exempts most people from a fundamental responsibility of citizenship but as a route to upward mobility is firmly grounded in racial and class inequality. Yet it can't be denied that conscription is the most naked form of state coercion an ordinary citizen can expect to face.

If in the face of these conundrums we aim to move as far as we can toward a defense based on popular, democratic participation, the discussion must transcend the strategic and begin with the broadly political. For surely the first requirement of such an undertaking is a foreign policy that is the product of genuine democratic deliberation—which in turn requires strong democratic institutions and a cultural ethos of democracy shared by citizens and the representatives they elect, including a lively, vigilant opposition from political factions and social movements not in power. We need, in short, a polity with built-in inhibitions against the abuses of authority that war or its threat invites.

Democracy of this sort, in America and elsewhere, has always been more aspiration than achievement, especially at the level of international relations. But at this point in our history, democracy, even as an aspiration, is in very deep trouble. The defense strategy that Scarry decries, and the autocratic foreign policies that go with it, have been around a long time, but at least during the Cold War and Vietnam years there were tumultous debates about those policies as well as about domestic political and cultural issues. Since 1989, however, Americans have been increasingly depoliticized. In the face of neoliberalism domestically and American triumphalism internationally, the left is paralyzed and adrift; as a result we are moving toward a form of one-party state. In this period the Republicans have effectively controlled the country, while the Democrats are no longer in any significant sense a party of opposition: when in power they imitate the Republicans, when out of power they wring their hands and defer. Before 9/11 a president who by any democratic criterion should not have held the office had already gotten the "opposition" to swallow John Ashcroft and a huge tax cut for the plutocracy. Now the congressional Democrats require only face-saving consultation before giving him his way on Iraq.

Right after 9/11 there was an interesting, indeterminate moment when social solidarity was in the air. A great many Americans seemed to share an impulse to express that solidarity by doing something, even if it was just displaying a flag. Media commentators debated about what the impulse meant: some, on both the left and the right, equated it with nationalist outrage; some, with disturbing alacrity, heralded a rejection of self-indulgent consumerist frivolity in favor of sobriety and sacrifice; still others hoped for a revival of the public's interest in politics, even a rethinking of market fundamentalism and a turn toward collective responsibility for pressing social needs. The moment soon passed, but not before it had made strikingly apparent that we are being governed by an administration so ideologically authoritarian it is allergic to any kind of popular mobilization, even in behalf of its own policies. George W. Bush has never asked Americans for anything but to go on about their business confident that he is fighting evil on our behalf. The administration launched no program to recruit Americans for civil defense (unless one counts Ashcroft's repugnant and tone-deaf proposal that meter readers and delivery people spy on the households they serve); issued no call for volunteer fighters in Afghanistan or civilian efforts to support the troops.

Of course, the game in Afghanistan was, as it has been in every war since Vietnam, to minimize the role of American soldiers on the ground and the direct stakes of the American people in the conflict. This strategy is always attributed to "American intolerance for casualties," as if that were some inherent national trait. But the more basic lesson of Vietnam, for the warmakers, was that discrepancies between government propaganda and battlefield experience spell big trouble. The Afghan intervention was popular even among many, like myself, who otherwise abhor the Bush-Cheney-Rumsfeld-Ashcroft axis: we saw it as a legitimate act of self-defense against an illegitimate, barbaric regime. Nonetheless the policy was to keep as much distance as possible between Americans and the nitty-gritty of war. Who knows? Closer involvement might have inspired an inconvenient sense of responsibility, a popular revulsion against our abdication to the thugs of the Northern Alliance and our shameful refusal to secure the peace.

I hope it's clear I'm not complaining that Bush isn't a better demagogue—all things considered we can be grateful for that. It's always crucial to distinguish between democracy and populism, and never more so than when trying to sort out rational from irrational fears and national defense from nationalist adventure. Yet it's more than unnerving to realize the extent of the administration's condescension toward the public—how irrelevant, really, it considers us. The rumor that Flight 93 was actually shot down may be false; it remains a resonant metaphor for the relationship of our present government to our historic self-conception.

3

REPLY

ELAINE SCARRY

Can we generalize about defense arrangements on the basis of a single day? A single morning? Steve Walt says we cannot.

On this one morning, 10 percent of all Manhattan office space was destroyed. Three sides of the formerly five-sided Pentagon were damaged. Three thousand lives were lost, the largest number of casualties on U.S. soil in a single day since the Battle of Antietam. Would we argue, if we were living in the aftermath of that September 1862 battle, that no conclusions should be drawn from that single day? People living at that time *did* draw conclusions. Civil War historian James McPherson has shown that as a result of that solitary day: 1) Lincoln issued the Emancipation Proclamation; 2) the war changed from a war over union to a war of liberation; and 3) France and Britain abandoned their support of the South.[1]

September 11 may prove to be equally pivotal, either turning the country further and further away from democracy (as in the Bush administration's abridgment of civil liberties, its pronouncements about the irrelevance of "evidence" in conducting twenty-first-century wars, its threats of "preemptive strikes" against "the axis of evil") or instead turning us back to our democratic foundations by its swift and stark exposure of the ineffectiveness of nondemocratic military arrangements.[2] Which way will we turn?

Many of the responses express regret for our departures from a democratic form of self-defense (both those departures that have gradually occurred over the last fifty years and those accelerated forms that have occurred since 9/11). At the same time, the responses together set forth a set of challenges about whether a democratic form of self-defense is achievable and desirable. The challenges come in three areas: first, the argument that international law, rather than democracy and constitutionalism, is the best safeguard against immoral and ineffective acts in war. Second, a set of questions about whether democracy (which abdicates force and requires openness) can ever be made compatible with war-making (which abdicates openness and requires force). Third, a collection of claims that self-defense is irrelevant because national security is no longer based on our own geographical borders and often occurs in distant spaces from which the citizenry is cut off.

First, then, the challenge from internationalism. Both democratic and international legal structures provide brakes on going to war. Neither is designed to eliminate war altogether; each is instead designed to minimize the chance of unjust wars, wars of aggression, or wars fought over issues that could be settled by other means. Two sets of brakes are obviously better than one or none; any act of war by the United States will ideally have both internal authorization

(Congress and the citizenry) and external authorization (the U.N.). But if only one of the two is relied upon, it must (in my view) be the democratic body of laws. Here is why.

First, most international treaties specify that nothing in the treaty should be construed as bypassing the constitutional requirements of the participating countries' own internal laws.[3] A U.N. sanction of war should never be understood as bypassing the need for congressional deliberation in the United States (Article I, Section 8) or deliberation by the citizenry (as required by the Second Amendment). It is important to stress this because presidents in the last several decades have generally assumed that 1) it is easier to get *legal sanction* for war from the U.N than from the U.S. Congress (despite the fact that in the autumn of 2002 Bush found Congress more compliant than the U.N); and 2) it is often easier to get *funding* for wars from international sources than from domestic ones (President Reagan, during the Iran-Contra affair, secretly sold weapons to Iran to raise money to support the Contras in Nicaragua, even though Congress had explicitly prohibited such support; President Bush Sr. funded 90 percent of the $60 billion Gulf War with funds from Germany, Japan, Kuwait, Saudi Arabia, and the United Arab Emirates).[4] Getting either legal authorization or money from inside the United States cannot be done without open debate, and open debate always allows testing, and testing allows dissent. Better to bypass dissent altogether.

It may be that in one hundred years the kind of "international democracy" that Richard Falk and Admiral Carroll envision will come into being,[5] but it cannot come into being if the "international forum" (which ordinarily requires the vote of a tiny number of persons) is used by world leaders to bypass the deliberative gates of their own nations (which entail the vote and voices of millions of people). Should an exception be made to address the genocidal events Paul Kahn worries about—Rwanda, East Timor, former Yugoslavia—where the injuries are so grave and the moral principles are so stark that cumbersome democratic gateways should be bypassed and international intervention initiated at once? But grave injuries and stark moral violations should be swiftly discernible in a democratic forum, if that forum has not atrophied from decades of disuse. Right now President Bush justifies his planned attack on Iraq by describing the country (which does not yet have a nuclear weapon) as an inevitable practitioner of genocide.

In the long run, we should work toward the following set of requirements. A country going to war ought to have to present its case in *both* democratic *and* international arenas. A negative vote in either arena should be sufficient to stop the war; formal authorization in both arenas should be required to go to war. This conforms to the general principle that "it ought always to be easier to make peace than to make war"—the principle that explains why, in United States law, the Senate acting alone can make a peace treaty but only the Senate and House acting together can make war.

The choice facing us in the present year is not, however,

whether to protect ourselves through democratic safeguards or instead through international safeguards since the first of those two—the democratic levers of self-protection—has moved beyond the reach of the citizenry. Before we can even be in a position to make such a choice the democratic model of self-defense will have to be reanimated. The question is do we wish to carry out that work of reanimation, or do we wish instead to rely for protection on monarchic weapons, unchecked executive war-making, and our present, authoritarian, top-down military arrangements.

I turn, then, to the second set of challenges, those that question whether the citizens of democracies can practice acts of self-defense without jeopardizing their own citizenship. This question is explicitly asked by Ellen Willis (who describes democracy and defense as oxymoronic on grounds of both force and secrecy), and is also indirectly introduced by other respondents (Kahn, Falk, Chayes, Walt) who refer in passing to the specter of "mob action" or citizen "excess."

Democracy has everything to do with peace; what has it to do with war? The heart of democracy is the agreement to divide responsibility for whatever injuring power the country has (whether none or a great deal) evenly across the full citizenry. This is why the distributive mandate embedded in the right to bear arms has been championed not only by militarists such as Mirabeau during the first General Assembly in France, but by pacifists such as Gandhi. Gandhi said, "Among the many misdeeds of the British rule in India, history will look upon the Act depriving a whole nation of arms as the blackest."[6] He argued that the population would decide whether or not to use its arms only after they were restored: in other words, the distributional right is prior to any question about whether a country will choose ever to use weapons.

Far from jeopardizing citizenship, the assuming of military responsibility has been the ground on which civil rights have been built in the United States. The Fifteenth Amendment, extending the right to vote to African-Americans, was inseparable from the military record: 180,000 blacks had fought in the Union Army, and this fact was repeatedly used in arguments supporting the new amendment in newspapers like the *Chicago Tribune* and the *New York Tribune,* on the floor of Congress, and in the 1868 presidential campaign. The Nineteenth Amendment, extending the vote to women, was achieved by suffrage songs, pageants, and plays, which repeatedly linked the capacity to vote with the capacity to serve in war. Finally, the Twenty-sixth Amendment, lowering the voting age from twenty-one to eighteen, was argued on a similar basis. Both the House and Senate judiciary hearings repeatedly cited the participation of those fighting in Vietnam and those deliberating about war on college campuses as having earned for their generation and all future generations the right to vote at a younger age.

This history provides strong support for those respondents who see the elimination of the draft as one of the key contributors to what Catherine Lutz calls the present era of "citizen passivity": Lutz and Knight explicitly focus on what happens when a draft is *absent*, and other respondents (Chayes, Willis) call attention to what happens when a draft is *present* by recalling the full stature of the citizenry (both those who fought and those who dissented) during the Vietnam period. With a draft in place, a president is obligated to address his countrymen and countrywomen with evidence supporting and justifying the country's military actions. The countrymen and -women not only determine whether the war will be fought but deliver a judgment about the credibility of the president's own leadership position.[7] Who dreads the draft? The population, to be sure, but even more so the executive heads of state who will at once lose their uncontested power to prosecute wars when and where they wish.

The anchoring of civil rights in military rights (in the history of the Fifteenth, Nineteenth, and Twenty-sixth Amendments) also provides support for the emphasis that respondents have placed on *concrete forms* of citizen participation in military matters other than the draft. Randy Forsberg directs attention to UrgentCall.org in the work of reducing U.S. reliance on nuclear weapons. Forsberg and Kahn remind us that Congress (however infantilized in recent decades by its refusal to carry out its gravest responsibility, the overseeing of our entry into war) can reassume its power at any moment it discovers the will to do so. And its will to do so, as Paul Kahn and Antonia Chayes point out, will be shaped by the actions of the citizens who communicate their arguments to the House and Senate.[8] *Concrete* questions require concrete answers from us. Should individual terrorists, Richard Falk asks, be identified as lone criminals (and judged within the framework of criminal rules) or instead as representatives of nations, thereby introducing the possibility of war?[9] Admiral Carroll, Antonia Chayes, and Richard Falk direct our attention to the pressing question of war against Iraq, a concrete question requiring from each of us a concrete answer.

The concrete levers of self-defense and self-government may be beyond the reach of the citizenry right now, but are they "out of reach" by a vast distance or instead by a gap so small it might be closed by a single day of concentrated stretching? The events of September 11—when the passengers on the Pennsylvania plane deliberated, voted, and acted in twenty-three minutes[10]—suggest that the gap is small, that the governing levers are there and within reach. Their being there, steadily within reach, is presumably what is meant by the words "gave proof through the night that the flag was still there." Does the phrase "the flag was still there" mean "our country can always out-injure any other country in an armed conflict"? Or does it instead mean "even in armed conflict we will keep recognizable and available to view the requirements of a civilian government"?

The third and final challenge is made up of a diverse array of objections, each of which points out that a citizens' defense is now, *practically speaking,* irrelevant. An egalitarian defense is irrelevant, practically speaking, because a population armed with conventional weapons cannot provide a shield against nuclear, chemical, or biological weapons. An egalitarian defense is irrelevant, practically speaking, because the U.S. military has a global presence and is stationed far from U.S. borders in countries about which our countrywomen and -men are ignorant. An egalitarian defense is irrelevant, practically speaking, because we protect ourselves today through long-term "security arrangements" in ways that are deterrents bound to future objectives and not to immediate acts of protection.

These three (and others like them) can be grouped together as the "challenge on the grounds of practical irrelevance." Each deserves to be scrutinized individually and debated at length, but for the purposes of this brief response let me direct attention to the major weakness they together share. Each makes a circular argument. Each of the three restates the fact that at present our country's defense is based on a centralized, authoritarian model that is severed from the population. That is precisely the problem that needs to be repaired; it is not an explanation for why we should abstain from the repair.

Our defense has been severed from the population by monarchic weapons that require only an executive order. Because we have long had nuclear weapons and acquired many new ones in the 1990s, other countries are now acquiring them, often explicitly justifying their acquisition by our example. Our ability to defend ourselves with conventional weapons (which at present, as Randy Forsberg notes, looks irrelevant) will become possible and relevant once all countries agree to rid themselves of nuclear weapons, an abolition that will take place only when the United States, the largest holder of them, initiates the global process of giving them up. It is, in other words, because we have authoritarian weapons that we are at present helpless against the possession of authoritarian weapons by others. And it is by returning to a democratic form of self-defense that we will create the world conditions that will eventually make that an effective form of self-defense. The return to a democratic form of self-defense is, as stressed earlier, prior to any question about *how much* defense the country will need. Whether the country's arsenal will be vast or instead minimal, interventionist or instead concentrated exclusively on homeland defense, are questions that can be answered by the citizenry once their authority over military matters has been restored.

Our defense has also been severed from the population by using the citizens' treasury not for protecting those citizens but for the project of dispersing the country's military force into foreign lands. Some respondents see this global dispersal as a legitimate form of security and others as instigating insecurity (Steve Walt sees it as both, listing it as evidence of our overall record of military success and as the probable incitement for the September 11 attacks). Whereas in the past, military leaders who lost battles were in danger of being fired, no one in the Department of Defense has been fired for the failures of September 11 because protecting the country is not part of the job description of the Department of Defense (which, for clarity, should perhaps be renamed the Department of Nonhomeland Defense or the Department of Global Empire). Citizens are kept from meddling in this global military dispersal not only by the geographical distance from their homes and temporal distance from the present (since the projects are often long-range) but also by the unavailability of information, portions of which are designated "top security."[11] If the country returns to a democratic self-defense, we should perhaps consider making our yearly funding of the Department of Defense contingent on a government-funded national debate on the role of the U.S. armed forces abroad. The Department of Defense ought to regard the population as a deliberative body in front of whom they need not only to report on, but to justify, their expensive undertakings.

These three challenges—the argument that the democratic should give way to the international, the argument that democracy and defense are incompatible, and the argument that democratic self-defense is irrelevant—do not in my view jeopardize the urgent importance of returning to a democratic self-defense, a return that some of the respondents agree with in full, some in part, and some not at all. Democratic arenas for deliberation about war can be greatly complemented (but never displaced) by international arenas. Civil rights—far from being jeopardized by military responsibilities—are premised on them. The reanimation of a democratic self-defense will alter the very features of our world that at present make that defense appear impractical.

In addition to these three key challenges, the respondents put forward many other important ideas and objections that deserve attention. I am grateful for all the responses and grateful that the New Democracy Forum has provided the space to begin to address the urgent question of our own obligations for defending the country, defending it against those who wish to injure its population, its skyline, or its democratic structures.

NOTES

ELAINE SCARRY / *Who Defended the Country?*

1. As with the matter-of-minutes vocabulary, the hairtrigger description is widely understood to apply either to the material act of firing a weapon or the mental act of deliberating. In the spring of 2001, Peace Links asked U.S. president Clinton and Russian president Putin to take all weapons off *"hair-trigger status,"* which gives "both countries *three minutes* to decide whether to launch nuclear missiles once the military tells them it thinks they have spotted an incoming missile." *South Bend Tribune,* April 29, 2001. Italics added. On "hairtrigger" arrangements throughout the last quarter of the twentieth century, see for example, the opening chapter of Daniel Ford, *The Button: The Pentagon's Strategic Command and Control System* (Simon & Schuster, 1985).

2. On the question of whether the country had a constitutional declaration of war against Iraq in the Gulf War, see Michael J. Glennon, "The Gulf War and the Constitution," *Foreign Affairs* 70 (Spring 1991): 84–101. The October 2002 "Authorization for the Use of Military Force Against Iraq" has key features which distinguish it from a congressional declaration of war.

3. Presidential First Use of Nuclear Weapons became a formal written policy in "Presidential Directive 59" during the Carter administration; it has been the country's official policy during the entire nuclear age. On Eisenhower's deliberations, for example, about using a nuclear weapon in the Taiwan Straits (1954) and again in Berlin (1959), see E. Scarry, "The Declaration of War: Constitutional and Unconstitutional Violence," in Austin Sarat and Thomas Kearns, eds., *Law's Violence,* Amherst Series in Law, Jurisprudence, and Social Thought (Univ. of Michigan Press, 1992), 23–77.

4. For example, President Bush Senior boasted, "I didn't have to get permission from some old goat in the United States Congress to kick [Iraqi president] Saddam Hussein out of Kuwait" (*Washington Post*, June 21, 1992, A18).

5. On the speed of Flight 77, see note 18 below.

6. "United States Department of Defense News Briefing," *M2 Press-wire* for September 17, 2001, states that it broke through the wall of corridor C, penetrating into the driveway that separates ring C from ring B (but it does not cite any damage to the B ring).

7. Angie Cannon, "The 'Other' Tragedy," *U.S. News and World Report* 131:24 (December 10, 2001), 22.

8. ABC News, September 14, 2001, described both the terrible burn injuries and the "wind of fire" spreading through the building. Angie Cannon in "The 'Other' Tragedy" gives an extended account of the injuries. Because no planes could fly into Washington, medical centers from around the country enlisted the help of marathon drivers to carry replacement skin: two drivers from Texas, according to Cannon, drove 70 square feet of skin to Washington in 23 hours and 12 minutes, stopping only for drive-through sandwiches and bathroom breaks; 30 square feet of skin arrived from Cincinnati in 12 hours; two surgeons at Washington Hospital Center, Dr. Marion Jordan and Dr. James Jeng, "worked 12- to 16-hour days" for three weeks.

9. The figure of 23,000 is given on the Pentagon Web site.

10. Three different times have been given for the crash of Flight 77 into the Pentagon: 9:38 A.M., 9:41 A.M., and 9:45 A.M. I cite the 9:45 A.M. time because it is given by many different reporters, both as a designation of the minute the plane "pierced" the Pentagon and as the minute interviewed eyewitnesses observed the impact, beginning on September 11 and 12 (CNN broadcasts throughout the afternoon of September 11; *Facts on File* for September 11, 2001; September 12 articles in the *New York Times, Newsday, Chicago Tribune, Atlanta Journal and Constitution, International Herald Tribune, Baltimore Sun*). In the weeks and months that followed, 9:45 A.M. continued to be used in multiple reports both within any single journal (*New York Times*, September 13, 15, 16, and November 4, 2001) and across many different journals (for example, *The New Yorker*, September 23; *Boston Globe*, November 23; *CNN Live*, December 15, 2001). The early time designation of 9:38 A.M. has been in-

troduced into the picture by the Pentagon (at first using the figure of 9:37 A.M.). On September 19, *Facts on File* noted: "the Defense Department placed [the crash] at 9:37 A.M. despite previous reports of 9:45 A.M."; and on the same day, the *New York Times* described 9:37 A.M. as the time "when the Pentagon estimates that the third hijacked jet crashed into the Pentagon." The Pentagon has had a series of commemorations, each beginning at 9:38 A.M. (starting with the three-month ceremony on December 11) and reporters have used this time in covering those events. But as the September through December publication dates listed above indicate, many journals and broadcasts have continued to use the 9:45 A.M. minute in describing the crash of the plane itself.

11. Presumably only the first of the two World Trade Center collisions was needed for the nation to know this second piece of information, that the seized planes would not land safely. But if one wants to base this knowledge on the destruction of both World Trade Center towers (hit at 8:47 A.M. and 9:02 A.M.), then the nation had forty-three minutes in which it knew that multiple planes were involved, that Flight 77 was likely to be one of the planes (since it had disappeared from radar even before the second tower was hit), and that no safe landing was likely.

12. Using the collision time of 9:38 A.M. (rather than 9:45 A.M.), the two periods would be *one hour fourteen minutes* and *forty-eight minutes.*

13. The times for the loss of radio and transponder are included in Glen Johnson's in-depth account, "Probe Reconstructs Horror," *Boston Globe,* November 23, 2001, 44–45.

14. At this point, American Airlines lacks any clear idea of the plane's location. At 9:09 A.M., American Airlines thinks Flight 77 may have gone into the second World Trade Center tower.

15. Barbara Olson also places a second call to the Justice Department several minutes later.

16. The timetable for both the air controllers' and pilots' sightings are given in Matthew L. Wald and Kevin Sack, "A Nation Challenged: The Tapes," *New York Times,* October 16, 2001, 1.

17. The exact flight path must by now have been precisely reconstructed, but it does not yet appear to be part of the public record. In any event, we know that the plane did not steadily circle Washington, D.C., or any other densely populated spot.

18. These mileage estimates are based on the supposition that Flight

77 was flying at the same 500-mph speed at which the World Trade Center planes were flying as they moved down the Hudson Valley at twice the legal airspeed (*New York Times*, October 16, 2001). Both air traffic controllers and the C-130 pilots described Flight 77 as "fast moving." (The *New York Times*, October 16, 2001, states that Flight 77 was moving at 500 mph when it hit the Pentagon. *U.S. News and World Report*, December 10, 2001, says the impact took place at a speed of 350 mph.)

19. See David Bond's detailed account in "Crisis at Herndon: 11 Airplanes Astray," *Aviation Week and Space Technology*, December 17, 2001, 96ff.

20. *New York Times*, October 16, 2001.

21. A retired official of the F.A.A. said, several days after the event, "There is no category of 'enemy airliners'" and added that he could recall no incident in which a military plane had ever intentionally attacked a civilian plane in the United States. (Matthew L. Wald, "After the Attacks: Sky Rules," *New York Times*, September 15, 2001, 1.) Major General Mike J. Haugen said that the crash of United Flight 93 initiated by the passengers "kept us from having to do the unthinkable . . . and that is to use your own weapons and own training against your own citizens" (*New York Times*, October 16, 2001).

22. Peter Beaumont, "Bin Laden in Plot to Bomb City: Terror Blueprint for Attack on London," *The Observer*, December 16, 2001, 1. Italics added.

23. Tim Ripley, "Global Army Controlled from a Suburban Bunker," *The Scotsman*, October 2, 2001, 6. Italics added.

24. Chris Buckland, "Meeting Hell with Horror," *News of the World*, September 30, 2001. Italics added.

25. The count of months and minutes here are the figures at the time this article first went to press with *Boston Review* (September 2002). As the article now goes to press in book form (January 2003) the count is fifteen months (648,000 minutes). Once the book appears in print, readers can supply a third set of figures, should the case remain unsolved.

26. For full analyses of the distributive intention of the right to bear arms see Elaine Scarry, "War and the Social Contract: Nuclear Policy, Distribution, and the Right to Bear Arms," *University of Pennsylvania*

Law Review 139 (May 1991): 1257–1316; and Akhil Reed Amar, *The Bill of Rights* (Yale Univ. Press, 1998), 46–63.

27. Most of the narrative details of Flight 93 that follow here as well as in Figure 2 come from two sources: "Forty Lives, One Destiny: Fighting Back in the Face of Terror," *Pittsburgh Post-Gazette,* October 28, 2001, a 6,000-word study; and "Final Words from Flight 93," *U.S. News and World Report* 131:18 (October 29, 2001), 32f, a story coauthored by Angie Cannon, Janet Rae-Dupree, Suzie Larsen, and Cynthia Salter. The passenger and crew quotations provided in these two in-depth news stories recur (with small variations) in Jere Longman, *Among the Heroes: United Flight 93 and the Passengers and Crew Who Fought Back* (Harper-Collins, 2002), a book which became available after the writing of this article was complete. It contains richly textured portraits of the thirty-seven passengers and seven crew (both their backgrounds and their actions on September 11). Although the book's purpose is to celebrate the passengers and crew of Flight 93, rather than to raise questions about U.S. defense, the preface notes that "they accomplished what security guards and military pilots and government officials could not" (p. x).

28. The overall time frame, from the moment the passengers first expressed their knowledge of the seizure at 9:31 A.M. to the moment the plane was on the ground at 10:10 A.M., is thirty-nine minutes: the reader may therefore wish to assess the sequence of steps in terms of thirty-nine rather than twenty-three minutes. I have used the twenty-three-minute frame because we only have information up through the moment the passengers collectively decided to act, not during the moments when control of the plane was wrestled over or during the time the plane fell toward the ground (the transcript of the voice recorder from the plane that would provide information about this period has so far been withheld from the public by the FBI).

29. In Jeremy Glick's case, family members used a second phone to contact the New York State Police, who then "patched in" to Jeremy Glick's phone call and listened to the ongoing descriptions of the hijacking he was giving.

30. The withholding of the plane's voice tape from the public has permitted rumors to exist that the military shot the plane down (despite consistent government statements that the military took no action). The

open passenger phone lines verify that quite apart from whatever the military did or did not do, the passengers themselves did act. The fact that government officials who have heard the plane's voice tape (most notably President Bush) have publicly celebrated the courage of the passengers reinforces what the public phone lines themselves already make clear.

31. Kanan Makiya and Hassan Mneimneh, translators and interpreters, "Manual for a 'Raid,'" in *New York Review of Books*, January 17, 2002, 18.

32. Perhaps more accurately, they are told that such matters are beyond their own agency: "All [the United States'] . . . equipment and all their gates and all their technology do not do benefit or harm except with the permission of God." In contrast, harm from resistant passengers is not left to God but is something the manual requires the hijackers to address.

33. They left a wide margin of safety: many miles of terrain still stood between the plane and whatever target in Washington or New York was the terrorists' destination.

34. A Coast Guard plane, already in the air, got close enough to instruct him by hand signals to land, but the boy declined to follow these instructions. See Brad Smith, "Skyscraper Hit," *Tampa Tribune*, January 6, 2002, 1.

35. Repeatedly questioned about "Rules of engagement" during a news briefing, Secretary of Defense Donald Rumsfeld declined to provide concrete answers: "The normal procedure is not to get into that subject in any detail" ("Federal Document Clearing House Political Transcript," September 27, 2001).

36. The events on the Pennsylvania plane clearly depended on the two-directional exchange of information between passengers and friends on the ground. There is probably a useful generalization that can be made here. Communication on planes between passengers and people on the ground should be made as easy as possible, since the most likely way passengers will get crucial information in an emergency is by being able to speak with friends or family. Emergency telephone links between passengers and government officials (FBI, FAA, Air Force, Pentagon) are much less likely to be helpful because in our present era

government officials do not believe in two-directional exchanges of information with citizens.

37. Congressional testimony explaining the cessation of round-the-clock flights (Operation Noble Eagle) focused on the expense in dollars ($50 million a week), in use of airmen (11,000 airmen in comparison with 14,000 airmen for the war in Afghanistan, according to the *New York Times*, March 18, 2002), and in wear and tear on the planes, rather than on the futility of this form of defense. However, the Air Force chief of staff testified to the Senate Armed Services Committee that air marshals inside the planes themselves were a more efficient solution than the fighter jets (Gen. John P. Jumper, March 7, 2002, Senate Armed Services Committee hearing). Because General Jumper was told by Senator Warner that he should give his assessment of the combat air patrols twice—first in a nonclassified and then in a classified form—we do not know his full thoughts on the matter.

38. For example, President Bush's June 1, 2002, graduation speech at West Point had three features which together seemed to make it an announcement (however blurry and genial) of the possibility of a nuclear first strike: it stressed preemptive action; it left the form of preemption (ground invasion, air strike) unspecified; and it explicitly summoned nuclear weapons, rejecting as inadequate and "too late" the Cold War strategy of "massive retaliation." Transcript, Federal News Service, June 1, 2002. Although immediate news coverage did not mention the word "nuclear," the phrases "first strike" and "preemptive first strike" were widely used in the United States (on ABC News, for example, where Sam Donaldson asked, "When do we take these other nations out?") and internationally (headlines for the *London Daily Telegraph*, *The Guardian*, *The Independent*, and *The Herald* of Glasgow all described President Bush as warning of a "first strike," and the *Financial Times* emphasized "pre-emptive, unilateral action").

39. Reed Hundt, "A Better Network for Emergency Communications," *New York Times*, December 25, 2001. Discussions of phone use during emergencies often pose the choice of whether we want citizens or instead firemen to have phone access. But during the days following September 11, there were many reports of both citizens and firemen having difficulty completing calls. According to an article in *Government*

Executive (October 2001), government executives (including financial leaders, federal executives, utility managers, and relief workers) had a 95 percent success rate in making calls during this period because they are beneficiaries of Government Emergency Telecommunication Service (GETS), which gives their calls priority over ordinary users of "AT&T, Sprint, and WorldCom."

40. For discusssion of the democratic structures violated by nuclear weapons see Elaine Scarry, "War and the Social Contract" and "Declaration of War." (See notes 3 and 26.)

41. See Paul Bracken, *Fire in the East: The Rise of Asian Military Power and the Second Nuclear Age* (HarperCollins, 1999), 64.

42. On the decoy problem, see Stephen Weinberg, "Can Missile Defense Work?" *New York Review of Books*, February 14, 2002: "The big problem, as it has been since the days of Nike X, is that any number of interceptor missiles could be used up in attacking decoys that had been sent by the attacker along with its warheads" (42); and Ted Postol, "What's Wrong with Missile Defense?" *Boston Review* 26:5 (October/November 2001), 40–45.

PAUL W. KAHN / *Democracy Won't Help*

For legal arguments on the interpretation of the War Powers clause see P. Kahn, "War Powers and the Millennium," *Loyola Law Review* 34 (November 2000).

CHARLES KNIGHT / *A Success of Democracy?*

1. Remarkably, the country's leadership has still not taken the most direct step toward protecting ourselves from this threat: placing very well-trained air marshals on every flight. Expensive? Yes, but also a sufficient defense to remove this weapon from the options available to terrorists.

NOTES

ANTONIA CHAYES / *An Informed Citizenry*

1. David Firestone and James Risen, "White House in Shift Backs Inquiry on 9/11," *New York Times,* September 21, 2002.

CATHERINE LUTZ / *The Slide into Passivity*

1. Catherine Lutz, *Homefront: A Military City and the American Twentieth Century* (Beacon Press, 2001).
2. Mary Kaldor, *The Baroque Arsenal* (Hill and Wang, 1981).
3. Robert W. McChesney, *Corporate Media and the Threat to Democracy* (Seven Stories Press, 1997).
4. Ann Markusen, Peter Hall, Scott Campbell, and Sabina Deitrick, *The Rise of the Gunbelt: The Military Remapping of Industrial America* (Oxford University Press, 1991); Joseph Masco, "States of Insecurity: Plutonium and Post–Cold War Anxiety in New Mexico, 1992–1996," in Jutta Weldes, et al., eds., *Cultures of Insecurity: States, Communities, and the Production of Danger* (Univ. of Minnesota Press, 1999).

RANDALL FORSBERG / *Citizens and Arms Control*

1. At the height of the Cold War, when nuclear weapons were being used to help deter a major East-West conventional war in Europe (by threatening escalation to a nuclear catastrophe), military officials argued that if we reduced or abolished nuclear weapons, we would have to increase the conventional armed forces needed to deter or fight in a war in Europe with the former Soviet Union, which had a huge army. This is no longer true.

ELAINE SCARRY / *Reply*

1. For these and other outcomes (such as Lincoln's act of relieving General McClellan of his command), see James M. McPherson, *Crossroads of Freedom: Antietam* (Oxford Univ. Press, 2002).
2. Was Antietam—with its ghastly death toll and its reconfiguration of winners and losers—just "a metaphor" (to cite Stephen Walt's often

repeated charge against my analysis)? The battle strategies and out-comes at Antietam were not just a metaphor, but neither are the two forms of defense displayed on September 11. It might relax us to think of Flight 77 and Flight 93 as two "metaphorical" ships of state. That would be a serious intellectual error. The two planes were certainly ships of state, but they were not metaphorical: the people on them were real, the methods of gathering or failing to gather information were real, the force exerted and the force not exerted against the terrorists were real, the lines of distributed or instead hierarchical authority were real, and perhaps most important, the presence (in the one case) and absence (in the other case) of consent were real. The two methods of defense they embody are alternatives everywhere throughout the country awaiting our judgment.

3. Without such a provision, the international bodies would be in danger of eviscerating or nullifying the very countries who are their members.

4. According to a 1991 House hearing on "Contributions to the Gulf War," the Gulf Crises Financial Coordination Group raised $54 billion from U.S. allies, including $5.5 billion from Germany, $4 billion from the United Arab Emirates, $13.5 billion from Saudi Arabia, $3.6 billion from Kuwait, and $9.4 billion from Japan. Transcript, "Hearing of the House Foreign Affairs Committee," May 14, 1991.

5. Emma Rothchild also persuades me that this is a reachable goal.

6. Mohandas K. Gandhi, *An Autobiography: The Story of My Experiments with Truth* (Beacon Press, 1993), trans. M. Desai.

7. Alexander Bickel writes, the antiwar movement succeeded in "top-pling a sitting president, in the midst of war, in 1968, before a single national vote had been cast." *The Morality of Consent* (Yale Univ. Press, 1975), 102–3.

8. Whether wholly *immune forms* of citizen participation—such as Kahn's reliance on public opinion—can work in isolation from *citizen risk* is one of many topics introduced by respondents that deserves extended debate.

9. Richard Falk argues that the statelessness of the terrorists might make democracy or nationhood an inappropriate forum of address. But it is precisely one of the tasks of Congress and the citizenry to determine—in cases where foreign citizens have injured the United States

citizens or interests—whether those foreign citizens have acted as individual agents or instead as soldiers of their countries. This was one of the issues, for example, debated by Congress during its deliberations leading up to the Mexican War of 1846 ("Deliberations for the Declaration of War against Mexico," *Congressional Globe,* 29th Cong., 1st session, 1846, 786–88, 800).

10. For a skeptical view of the passengers' work, see the essay by Charles Knight.

My essay argued that September 11 called into question a central argument used to legitimize the centralization of military power over the last fifty years, namely the argument from speed. Several respondents have questioned whether the subject of speed has been key during the decades of massive centralization. Because of length constraints on my writing of this brief response, I must postpone counterarguments to a later time; and here ask only two questions. Is the "matter of minutes" vocabulary (as in the passages I cited concerning Prime Minister Blair) unfamiliar or instead long familiar to readers? Second, aren't such descriptions often linked to a solitary executive actor? Peter Raven-Hansen summarizes the often-made argument: "If there are only minutes in which to decide to use nuclear weapons, Congress cannot possibly participate. In these circumstances, the President must be conceded inherent nuclear decision-making authority." "Nuclear War Powers," *American Journal of International Law* 83:4 (October 1989), 790.

11. Although the Secretary of Defense issues an annual report that describes the country's military undertakings abroad, many kinds of information are withheld. Many genres of military information are difficult to obtain even when U.S. soil or coastal waters are involved: for example, announcements of military exercises along the coastlines are almost never issued to the public before or after they occur; obtaining information about the nature of the exercise or the craft used requires the filing of Freedom of Information requests that result in only sketchy information.

ABOUT THE CONTRIBUTORS

Rear Admiral Eugene J. Carroll, Jr., U.S. Navy (Ret.), served in the Navy for thirty-seven years. His assignments included command of the Carrier Striking Force of the U.S. Sixth Fleet and the direction of U.S. military operations in Europe and the Middle East under General Alexander Haig.

Antonia Chayes teaches at Harvard's Kennedy School and served as U.S. Air Force undersecretary.

Richard Falk is Albert G. Milbank Professor of International Law and Practice and professor of politics and international affairs at Princeton University, and author most recently of *Predatory Globalizaton.*

Randall Forsberg is director of the Institute for Defense & Disarmament Studies in Cambridge, Massachusetts.

Paul W. Kahn is Robert W. Winner Professor of Law and Humanities at Yale Law School. His most recent works include *The Cultural Study of Law* and *Law and Love.*

Charles Knight is a defense policy analyst with the Project on Defense Alternatives (PDA) at the Commonwealth Institute, Cambridge, Massachusetts. His current work addresses issues of preemptive war.

Catherine Lutz is a professor of anthropology at the University of North Carolina, Chapel Hill. She is author of *Unnatural Emotions, Reading National Geographic* (with Jane Collins), and *Homefront.*

Elaine Scarry, Walter M. Cabot Professor of Aesthetics and the General Theory of Value at Harvard University, is author of *The Body in Pain, On Beauty and Being Just,* and many articles on war and social contract.

ABOUT THE CONTRIBUTORS

STEPHEN M. WALT is academic dean at the John F. Kennedy School of Government, where he holds the Robert and Renee Belfer Professorship in International Affairs.

ELLEN WILLIS, a former staff writer for *The New Yorker* and the *Village Voice*, is director of the cultural reporting and criticism program at New York University and author of *Don't Think, Smile!*